The Suspended Middle

The Suspended Middle

Henri de Lubac and the
Debate concerning the Supernatural

JOHN MILBANK

SCM PRESS

LONDON

© 2005 Wm. B. Eerdmans Publishing Co.

British Library of Cataloguing in Publication Data

A catalogue record for this book is available
from the British Library

ISBN 0 334 04045 0

First published 2005 in the United States of America by
Wm. B. Eerdmans Publishing Co.
255 Jefferson Ave. S.E., Grand Rapids, Michigan 49503
and in the U.K. by
SCM Press
9-17 St. Albans Place, London N1 0NX

www.scm-canterburypress.co.uk

SCM Press is a division of SCM-Canterbury Press Ltd

Printed and bound in the United States of America

In memory of my Maternal Grandparents

James Baxter Maclagan ⚘ *1901–1967*
Jane Brown Maclagan ⚘ *1900–2003*

Alba gona hiongantaibh
Scotland with its wonders

CONTENTS

INTRODUCTION

For what we do by means of our friends, is done in a sense, by ourselves.

> Aristotle, cited by Aquinas with reference
> to the paradox of grace and the natural
> human orientation to the supernatural[1]

Moreover, this concept of a pure nature runs into great difficulties, the principal one of which seems to me to be the following: how can a conscious spirit be anything other than an absolute desire for God?

> Henri de Lubac, in a letter to
> Maurice Blondel, April 3, 1932[2]

1. Aristotle, *Ethics* iii. 3, cited by Aquinas at *Summa Theologiae* (hereafter ST) I-II. Q.5, a4 ad 1.
2. Cited by Lawrence Feinberg, *The Natural Desire to See God according to St. Thomas and His Interpreters* (Rome: Apollinare Studi, 2001), p. 628.

Introduction

Others destroy the gratuity of the supernatural order, since God, they say, cannot create intellectual beings without ordering and calling them to the beatific vision.

Humani Generis, August 12, 1950[3]

Le Surnaturel, c'est du réel précis.

Robert Bresson, film director[4]

The above sequence of quotations traces in outline the theological and personal drama of the life of Henri de Lubac. In the first, we have the patristic and high mediaeval paradox of the supernatural which de Lubac sought to recover: that which is wholly done for us by God, namely deification by grace, is yet also our highest act and as such properly our own — even that which is most properly our own.

The second encapsulates Henri de Lubac's core theological belief, based upon this paradox — stated clearly here in private correspondence, but almost never so distinctly in his published writings — namely that there *is* no

3. *Humani Generis*, in *The Papal Encyclicals, 1939-58*, ed. Claudia Carlen (Raleigh: McGrath, 1981), pp. 175-85, 26.
4. Cited by P. Georges Chantraine, S.J., in his article "Le Surnaturel: Discernement de la Pensée Catholique selon Henri de Lubac" in *Revue Thomiste, Surnaturel* special issue (Jan.-June 2001): 31-50. The citation is on page 50 and includes also the following: "'Traduire le vent par l'eau qu'il sculpte. . . . Quand j'écrivais ces lignes, je ne pensais pas à l'Esprit Saint, j'étais réaliste. Mais peut-on échapper au reel? C'est parce que jè suis réaliste que je crois en Dieu et du mystères.'"

spiritual, intelligent being (angelic or human) that is not ordered by grace to the beatific vision: that is, to deification.

The third, with equal clarity, shows papal rejection of such a view, which was considered to be lurking in de Lubac and many others. Defenders of de Lubac who deny that he was implicated in this statement by Pius XII are surely wrong, and critics who insist that he was, are surely correct. Yet this of course leaves the theological issue open: it is hard to read de Lubac's penultimate book, *Pic de la Mirandole,* written when he was eighty, without reaching the conclusion that he covertly opposed this paragraph of *Humani Generis* to the end of his life.

The fourth, and most profound and comprehensive, reminds us that de Lubac's opinion, however controversial, informed a new sensibility which stood at the heart of the Catholic cultural revival in the twentieth century.

1

The Life and Writings
of Henri de Lubac

Henri de Lubac was a Jesuit theologian, educated at Jesuit centers in France and England before the First World War.[1] (Unlike some of his *confrères*, he received no other formal academic training.) In that war he suffered a serious wound in the head, a wound which affected him somewhat throughout his long life. In the inter-war years, he was the central but sometimes shadowy figure of a diverse new theological movement in France which called for a rejection of neo-scholasticism and for a tempering of the scholastic stress upon speculation with a renewed interest in history, biblical exegesis, typology, art, literature, and mysticism.

---

1. For more information relevant to this chapter, see Hans Urs von Balthasar, *The Theology of Henri de Lubac: An Overview* (San Francisco: Ignatius, 1991), and Étienne Fouilloux, "Henri de Lubac au moment de la Publication de *Surnaturel*," in *Revue Thomiste, Surnaturel* [hereafter RT *Surnaturel*], special edition, no. I-II (January-June 2001): 13-30; Aidan Nichols O.P., "Thomism and the *Nouvelle Théologie*," in *The Thomist* (January 2000): 1-19; Fergus Kerr, *After Aquinas: Versions of Thomism* (Oxford: Blackwell, 2002), pp. 53-56, 128ff., 147, 208; *Immortal Longings* (Notre Dame, IN: Notre Dame University Press, 1997), pp. 158-85.

(Other important names are Jean Daniélou, M.-D. Chenu, Henry Bouillard, Yves Congar, and Gaston Fessard.) The initial aim was *ressourcement* — a recovery of the riches of Christian tradition, especially prior to 1300. The eventual aim though, was a renewal of speculative theology in a new mode that would restore its closeness to the exegetical, mystical, and liturgical reading of revealed signs. With the publication of *Catholicisme* in 1938, de Lubac produced one of the key texts of this movement: the book stressed the social character of the Church as the true universal community in embryo, rather than as a mere external machinery for the saving of individual souls.[2] Accordingly it encouraged an open yet critical engagement with the world. Already here, one of the 'paradoxical' axes of de Lubac's thought was apparent: "Catholic" expresses a reach of divine grace that is all-encompassing — to the entire past and future and all of space, worldly and cosmic, extending beyond the explicit profession of Christianity. Yet at the same time, "Catholic" means a universality whose grammar is only fully spelled out in the life of the incarnate *Logos*. Within this harmonious tension, the sway of de Lubac's first and last master — Origen of Alexandria — is always apparent. Likewise evident is the practical missionary concern fused with intellectual rigor and unwillingness to compromise on essentials of a Jesuit father.

If this follower of St. Ignatius was at all a saint, it was in a wholly militant mode. For all his reticence, de Lubac's writings often exhibit a withering aristocratic disdain of

2. *Catholicism: Christ and the Common Destiny of Man*, trans. Lancelot C. Sheppard (London: Burns and Oates, 1937).

philistine opponents, and for all the commitment to patient and exhaustive scholarship, his deliberate selection of august targets and coordinated intellectual strategy is often to the fore. Twice he was engaged in secular warfare: once, as noted, under the drastic *aegis* of the French Republic which made no exemptions from military service for religious (a fellow Jesuit, and enormous intellectual influence, Pierre Rousselot, was killed in the trenches); later, during WWII, on the run from the Vichy regime and subsequently the Gestapo. At the time that he was composing his *Surnaturel* (arguably the key theological text of the twentieth century) he was also in touch, along with his fellow Jesuits of the School at Lyon, with the Gaullist resistance.[3] His *confrère* and intellectual collaborator Yves de Montcheuil was captured and martyred by the Gestapo. And it is vital to grasp that de Lubac's and de Montcheuil's *political* opponents — Catholic Rightists supporting the Vichy regime and collaborating with the occupying Germans — were also their *theological* opponents, who reported what they regarded as dubious theological opinions as well as their dubious secular involvements back up the chains of Jesuit and Dominican command to Rome itself. (It should be stressed though, that de Lubac's enemies in the French Catholic hierarchy were often well to the right of Pius XII and his advisors in the Vatican.)

Surnaturel was an intentional body blow to the neo-

---

3. *Surnaturel: Études Historiques: nouvelle édition* (Paris: Desclée de Brouwer, 1991). There is as yet — shockingly — no English translation of this text. Although much of the same material is revisited in the translated works cited in note 9, below, these works substantially modify — under pressure — the earlier book.

scholastic understandings of reason and grace, as well as to neoscholastic conceptions of philosophy and theology and the relation between them. It was not that it advocated a particular view on a particular theological topic; it was rather that it implicitly (indeed in an almost coded fashion) dismantled the entire set of reigning Catholic (and perhaps Protestant) assumptions about the character of Christian intellectual reflection. Moreover, it did so not in the name of innovation but of an authentic tradition which it sought to recover.

Most of de Lubac's other writing, which in a sense works out the thesis of *Surnaturel* in relation to ecclesiology, exegesis, inter-religious dialogue, and secular social and scientific thought, is of a similar character. It does not often contribute directly to the detailed development of doctrine. Nor, on the other hand, does it directly contribute to a metaphysical or a foundational theology. Rather, it offers something like a 'grammar' of Christian understanding and practice, both for the individual and the community. I think that the word 'grammar' is appropriate, yet it poses a trap for the English-speaking reader. In keeping with his double Jesuit vocation to the practical and the theoretical-contemplative, and in line with his immediate intellectual precursor, Maurice Blondel, de Lubac's pragmatic bent — his desire to set out "directions for the regulation of Christian ingenuity" (to echo Descartes) — was entirely bound up with an equal measure of visionary *élan*. The grammar of Christian life was re-envisaged; so too was ontology itself.

This absolutely fundamental aspect of his work can, however, elude the reader. After all, have I not just said that de Lubac did *not* ever construct a metaphysic or pursue a speculative dogmatics? So what room for ontology is there here, if he offered neither a philosophical metaphysics, nor a revisionary one based upon faith? The answer is that he implicitly proposed a new sort of ontology — indeed, in a sense a 'non-ontology' — articulated *between* the discourses of philosophy and theology, fracturing their respective autonomies, but tying them loosely and yet firmly together. (The paradoxical expression 'non-ontology' seems appropriate because, strictly speaking, the word 'ontology' was first used in the early seventeenth century to denote a purely philosophical classification of being, cognitively prior to a consideration of the divine.)

This 'non-ontology' de Lubac saw as the return of authentic Christian discourse, which could be indifferently described as 'Christian philosophy' or as 'sacred doctrine'. By 'non-ontology' (my term) I must stress that I do not mean that de Lubac refused ontology: rather I mean that he articulated an ontology between the field of pure immanent being proper to philosophy on the one hand, and the field of the revelatory event proper to theology on the other.

This new ontological discourse concerned the paradoxical definition of human nature as intrinsically raised above itself to the 'super-nature' of divinity. Since, as we shall see, for de Lubac all created nature was in some sense orientated to human nature, this paradoxical structure even extended to the constitution of all finite beings as such.

For de Lubac the enigma ran equally in two opposite directions. On one hand, the extra-ordinary, the supernatural, which is always manifest within the Creation, is present at the heart of the ordinary: it is "precisely the real" — or 'the real in its precision' — as Bresson put it. On the other hand, the ordinary and given always at its heart points beyond itself and in its spiritual nature aspires upwards to the highest. Grace is always kenotic; the natural is always elevated but not destroyed. Yet by a symmetrical paradox the 'more' that is demanded by nature can only be received from God as a gift.

After WWII de Lubac further worked out this twofold paradox of grace in the realms of ecclesiology and sacramental theology (*Corpus Mysticism,* 1944), biblical exegesis (*Exégèse Médiévale,* 1959-64),[4] and in reflection on the evolutionary theory of his friend Teilhard de Chardin.[5] One of the most attractive aspects of de Lubac's personality was his willingness to defend and refine the position of Teilhard, even though he thought that at times it verged on heresy. This same sympathy for marginal Christian or non-Christian thinkers whom he felt might be more profoundly near the heart of Christian truth than more 'orthodox' ones, de Lubac applied also to thinkers of the past — to Origen himself, to Pico, to Proudhon, and to Buddhist philosophers.

In the post-war years the battle with the Christian political right had been won, but not that with ecclesiastical conservatism. Although de Lubac enjoyed initial papal sympathy, neo-scholastic forces in his own order brought him

4. *Corpus Mysticum: L'Eucharistie et L'Eglise au Moyen Age* (Paris: Aubier-Montaigne, 1949). A translation of this work into English is in progress. Henri de Lubac, *Exégèse Médiévale: Les Quatres sens de L'Écriture* (Paris: Aubier, 1940). This is in four volumes. The first two volumes have appeared (with the other two projected) as *Medieval Exegesis: The Four Senses of Scripture,* volume 1 translated by Mark Sebanc, volume 2 by E. M. Macierowski (Grand Rapids/Edinburgh: Eerdmans/T&T Clark, 1998 and 2000).

5. Amongst several other books, see Henri de Lubac, *Teilhard de Chardin: The Man and His Meaning,* trans. René Hague (New York: Hawthorn, 1965).

under papal suspicion, and following upon the publication of the encyclical *Humani Generis* (1950) he was forbidden to teach or publish for several years. Gradually however, he and fellow exponents of what was now dubbed by their enemies the *nouvelle théologie* moved back not simply into favor but into the vanguard. De Lubac played a role in Vatican II: its pronouncements are regarded in contemporary scholarship as reflecting unresolved battles and partial compromises amongst the proponents of the *nouvelle théologie,* neo-Thomism, and a liberal accommodation to modernity.[6]

Indeed, soon after the Council, de Lubac was once more out of favor, this time for his criticism of the bureaucratic diminution of the authority of local bishops.[7] He was not made a cardinal until near the end of his life. After *Humani Generis,* outside his historical work, de Lubac comes across as a stuttering, somewhat traumatized theologian, only able to articulate his convictions in somewhat oblique fragments. He failed ever to write his proposed Bérulle-like theological-historical-mystical treatise on Christ or his projected history of mysticism. These two books, which he intended to be his central contribution, are missing from the heart of his *oeuvre.* He himself disarmingly said that some sort of spiritual failing rendered him incapable of expressing his views except through the interpretation of the views of others.[8]

---

6. See Tracey Rowlands, *Culture and the Thomist Tradition after Vatican II* (London: Routledge, 2003).

7. Hans Urs von Balthasar, *The Theology of Henri de Lubac,* pp. 113-14.

8. See Michael Sales's foreword to *Henri de Lubac: Theology in History* (San Francisco: Ignatius, 1996), p. 12.

Yet it is clear that this incapacity became more chronic after *Humani Generis*. De Lubac *did* continue to express certain views in his own voice, yet unlike the earlier case of *Catholicism*, his *crucial* views were now always expressed indirectly, through historical interpretations. His reaction to the encyclical remains a subject of intense debate and as we shall see below, it is arguable that it provoked in him severe theoretical incoherence. Sections of the *Surnaturel* were reworked as *Augustinisme et Théologie Moderne* and *Le Mystère du Surnaturel* (both 1965).[9] In these works, de Lubac, in response to *Humani Generis*, offers certain crucial qualifications to his understanding of the supernatural, most notably in relation to the question of whether there could be a spiritual nature *not* oriented towards grace. He now allows that, formally speaking, there could be. However, the view that this betokens any real shift in opinion runs into three interpretative problems: first of all, de Lubac had already conceded this point in the 1949 essay "Le Mystère du Surnaturel," antedating the encyclical.[10] (Claims, however, that the latter actually echoes de Lubac's wording seem disingenuous, if taken to imply an entire absence of tension between Pius XII and the *nouvelle théologie*.) In the second place, the 'concession' in this essay, which was expanded as chapters four and five of the book of the same name, is counterbalanced by yet more stringent arguments (as compared with *Surnaturel* itself) to the effect that this allowance

---

9. *Augustinianism and Modern Theology*, trans. Lancelot Sheppard (New York: Herder & Herder, 1969); *The Mystery of the Supernatural*, trans. Rosemary Sheed (London: Herder & Herder, 1967).

10. Henri de Lubac, "The Mystery of the Supernatural," in *Theology in History*, pp. 281-317.

does *not* (as the official position insists) guarantee the gratuity of grace. In the third place (as will be later shown), de Lubac's late work *Pic de la Mirandole* seems to provide, obliquely, his most radical statement yet of his fundamental and long-standing thesis.

In its general implications this thesis can be summed up thus: "Christianity is a humanism, else it is misunderstood. On the other hand, secular humanism is the absolute antithesis of the Gospel." The *Pico* book gives the sharpest account of this tension and in its deepened advocacy of a Christian humanism shows no sign whatsoever of a conservative dotage that would tend to emphasize the ecclesiastical transmission of faith, as distinct from its cultural embeddedness.

Indeed, there is no justification for an account of de Lubac and von Balthasar which suggests that they first embraced and then ultimately abandoned a youthful radicalism open to post-Kantian philosophy, which they shared with Karl Rahner and others in the tradition of Joseph Maréchal.[11] They were never simply or crudely *opposed* to this tradition of 'transcendental Thomism', but (as we shall see later) they interpreted its *very Kantianism* as still half-stuck in a false neo-scholastic legacy (though admittedly also half-escaping it). Accordingly, de Lubac's and von Balthasar's version of the claim that angels and humans possess an ineluctable natural destiny for the beatific vision was always *stronger* than that of Rahner, even if, equally,

---

11. See, for example — a particularly uninformed one — James Hanvey S.J., "Conclusion: Continuing the Conversation" in *Radical Orthodoxy: A Catholic Enquiry?* ed. Lawrence Paul Hemming (Aldershot: Ashgate, 2000), pp. 76-97.

their (still somewhat ambivalent) suggestions of a reach of influence of grace and revelation into all actual nature were stronger as well. They always — early and late — insisted on the *paradox* of the *surnaturel:* this insistence could appear to the ecclesiastical authorities at once 'radically' to threaten the gratuity of the supernatural and the revealed order, and 'conservatively' to threaten the autonomy of the natural domain of reason. But to imagine that the tension was earlier a matter of radicalism and later a matter of conservatism is certainly wrong for de Lubac — though with von Balthasar the issue is slightly more complex (see below). From *Surnaturel* onwards, de Lubac blamed the loss of the true doctrine of the supernatural for the emergence of a false idea of a 'purely natural' human domain which becomes the space of the secular and of modern philosophy, including Kantian philosophy — whose criticism of metaphysics de Lubac briefly dismisses as wholly dependent on a false and limited Newtonian construal of causality.[12] De Lubac's genealogy of the secular received its fullest expression in *Le Drame de l'Humanisme Athée* (1942) which (significantly) appeared two years before *Surnaturel* (von Balthasar's condemnation of Kant and idealism as one manifestation of 'titanism' also belongs to the earliest stratum of his own work).[13]

All the above suggests that de Lubac's increasing indirection after 1950 reflected both a continuing trauma and a

12. Henri de Lubac, *The Discovery of God [Les Chemins de Dieu]*, trans. Alexander Dru (New York: P. J. Kennedy, 1960), p. 65.

13. *The Drama of Atheist Humanism*, trans. E. M. Riley, A. E. Nash, and M. Sebanc (San Francisco: Ignatius, 1995). The book, however, focuses on the end of the story — on Feuerbach, Comte, and Nietzsche.

continued need for caution, even into his old age, despite his resonance with some 'conservative' ecclesiastical themes: opposition to a debased liturgy, to bureaucratic rule, and to obeisance before secular norms.

Yet there may be also a deeper reason for de Lubac's failure (if it is counted such) often to write in his own voice. In effect, the *surnaturel* thesis *deconstructs* the possibility of dogmatic theology as previously understood in modern times, just as it equally deconstructs the possibility of philosophical theology or even of a clearly autonomous philosophy *tout court*. For now, on the one hand, doctrine remains 'extrinsic', arbitrary, and incomprehensible unless interpreted in accordance with an innate, radically given human nature. The positive foundations of theology (its *topoi*) are no longer sufficient to determine the range of its conclusions. On the other hand, this 'given' human nature is only manifest to philosophy as paradoxically exceeding itself; later de Lubac denied that it is ever apparent at all, with any clarity, to reason alone. Philosophy then appears to require the transcendent supplement of theology, yet theology equally requires the (consequently non-available) foundation of philosophy. As the neo-Thomist critics understandably bewailed, de Lubac's paradox looks less like paradox than irresolvable *aporia*. With great accuracy, von Balthasar described de Lubac's writing as occupying a problematic "suspended middle."[14]

---

14. Hans Urs von Balthasar, *Henri de Lubac*, p. 15. Balthasar's summary here is wonderfully accurate: "De Lubac soon realized that his position moved into a suspended middle in which he could not practice any philosophy without its transcendence into theology, but also any theology without its essential inner structure of philosophy." The question is, did von Balthasar himself to some

And arguably, de Lubac's literary production reflects this *aporia* in its expansive and untidy character. De Lubac elaborated a "discourse of the supernatural" that was neither dogmatics nor philosophical theology — although he would have insisted that it represented a restoration of an Augustinian "Christian philosophy" or a Thomist *Sacra Doctrina*. It usually took the (only partially apparent) form of a historical theology. Such a form was inevitable in so far as a combination of event and sign in continuous process would seem to be the only possible ground that de Lubac's paradoxical discourse can occupy. De Lubac indeed declared that theology should be a mysticism and that mysticism was essentially a reading of signs. In the 1960s he even appealed to the semiotic vogue against humanism: since we are ruled by signs it is as rational to read, with Origen, St. Luke's publicans as angels, as it is, suspiciously, to read angels as publicans — as humanist modernity would encourage.[15] On the other hand, the relative absence of dogmatics and metaphysics in de Lubac also reflects a confinement to *ressourcement* and a failure to proceed to a newly enhanced 'speculation' on the part of a thinker at once traumatized and forced to speak always with caution.

Here, however, it is impossible to discuss the work of de Lubac without considering its relation to that of his slightly younger pupil, Hans Urs von Balthasar. It is tempting to think of von Balthasar as supplying just the new mode of

---

degree see such suspension as an *aporia* that froze all discourse? Does he always remain in this suspension, or does he himself practice some philosophy before theology and some theology in a 'mythical' mode beyond philosophy? See the discussion following.

15. *The Discovery of God*, p. 94.

speculation lacking in de Lubac himself. And to a large extent, this is correct. As Gilbert Narcisse complains, but others celebrate, von Balthasar's work in his great trilogy often seems to lack either philosophical or theological foundations.[16] It too occupies a "suspended middle"; it too seems to articulate a 'non-ontology'. Von Balthasar also continued the effort to expound an 'ontological grammar' of Christian practice by thinking about the transmutation of our sense of beauty, of drama, and of logic effected by the irruption of the *Logos* in history. More explicitly than de Lubac he saw that the 'middle' sphere of continuous event and sign is precisely the sphere of culture. He also was a Christian humanist; without Christian culture, he argued, there is only a nominal, not a mediated grace, which must remain uncomprehended and without real effect.

Nevertheless, as we shall see, von Balthasar at times also compromises the "suspended middle." His concessions to *Humani Generis* were arguably more real and substantial than those of de Lubac, as evidenced in the way his work more readily assumes the idioms of metaphysics, foundational theology, and positive dogmatics. This is no mere formal contrast: a corresponding substantive difference emerges in the way von Balthasar's dogmatics seems to float free of ontological conceptualization into a 'mythical' realm that is highly voluntarist and personalist, and in the end at times only tendentiously orthodox. It emerges also in contrasting attitudes to the Renaissance: de Lubac's praise of Pico, Cusa, and Bérulle is far more unstinting

16. Gilbert Narcisse, "Le Surnaturel dans la théologie Contemporaine," in RT *Surnaturel*, pp. 312-28.

than von Balthasar's. Where the latter saw a seed of 'titanism', the former saw a valid extension of patristic anthropocentrism. De Lubac was, in the end, at once more strictly orthodox *and* more radically humanistic. For as will be later argued, where von Balthasar celebrated in the end the spectacle of a divine gnostic drama, de Lubac, like Bérulle (and like Bulgakov), pointed towards the serene eternity of the God-Man.

2

The Surnaturel *of* 1946

De Lubac's most famous and controversial book was a some-what *ad hoc* jamming together of several earlier long articles which nonetheless converged upon a single thesis. Tracing the origin of the terms *hyperphues* and *supernaturalis,* de Lubac shows that, following pagan antiquity, they had first of all simply denoted the realm of the divine above that of known *physis.*[1] The Christian usage, referring to an intrusion of the divine within the cosmos and to an elevation of humanity, was cognate both with a new sense of *pneuma* (after Paul and Origen) to mean the deepest part of the human being that retains a profound ontological kinship with the divine origin, and with the new Christian understanding of

---

1. Henri de Lubac, *Surnaturel.* (See Chapter 1, note 3 above.) For the following summary, see the whole book and note especially the statement on p. 483: *"L'esprit est donc désir de Dieu."* See also the earlier works by Henri Bouillard, "L'idée de surnaturel et le Mystère Chrétien" in *L'Homme devant Dieu,* vol. 3 (Paris: Aubier-Montaigne, 1964), pp. 153-66; *Conversion et grace chez Thomas d'Aquin* (Paris: Aubier-Montaigne, 1944) [first published about the same time as *Surnaturel*]. In addition, for a very good summary and supplementation of all this research and argument, see Olivier Boulnois's article "Surnaturel" in *Dictionnaire Critique de Théologie,* ed. J.-Y. Lacoste (Paris: PUF, 1998).

salvation as deification, or ontological transformation into as close a likeness with God as is consistent with a persisting created status. These conceptual affinities are important, because they show that de Lubac, like Jean Daniélou, wished to stress that the original and authentic Latin patristic understanding of the operation of grace (especially that of Augustine) was not essentially different from the Greek patristic notion of deification.

According to de Lubac, a break with such an understanding had only occurred in late mediaeval and early modern scholasticism: first with Denys the Carthusian and then decisively with Cajetan. The latter, in de Lubac's view, inaugurated a new reading of Aquinas on grace which has come to dominate all later theology. According to this reading, when Aquinas speaks, in several passages, of a *desiderium naturale* or even a *desiderium naturae* in angels and humans for God (unlike neo-Thomism, as de Lubac pointed out), this does not denote an 'innate' desire in us for the beatific vision, a kind of deep ontological thrust, prior to any reflection. Instead, it merely denotes an 'elicited' desire, which is *purely of the will,* although occasioned by a curiosity proper to the intellect. We behold the effects of creation and desire by a mere vague *velleity* fully to know what has caused them. Thus we in no way remotely anticipate, by an ineradicable mystical bias, the true substance of the beatific vision.

But more precisely, Cajetan dealt with Thomas's "natural desire for the supernatural" by an intellectual "divide and conquer" strategy.[2] On the one hand, he suggests, be-

---

2. See also Henri de Lubac, *The Mystery of the Supernatural,* trans. Rosemary Sheed (London: Herder & Herder, 1967), pp. 48-67.

fore the call of grace, besides the 'elicited' natural desire, there is a mere *potentia obedientialis* of the human to the divine will. On the other hand, an authentic natural desire for the supernatural arises only with the grant of grace — which, it is important to stress, was, even for Cajetan, in *actuality* always present, both before the Fall and after it. In addition, Cajetan felt that he had to render Aquinas consistent by elaborating a doctrine of 'pure nature' which would alone do justice to the latter's doctrine of the gratuity of grace and his repeated distinction between what is due to humanity by nature and what accrues to him by free supernatural addition. Thus Cajetan, unlike Aquinas, explicitly says that human nature in *actuality* is fully definable in merely natural terms. This means that there can be an entirely natural and adequate ethics, politics, and philosophy and so forth. Man might even offend the moral law, and yet not be directly guilty of sin.

All later scholasticism rang changes upon these themes, with no essential dissent, right down to the early twentieth century. De Lubac, however, in *Surnaturel,* along with several others at the time, denied that this was a true reading of Aquinas. The angelic doctor's position on this issue remains today an interpretative crux, for no merely adventitious reasons — as will presently be explained.

In his historical tracing of the meaning of the word "supernatural," de Lubac further noted that, despite the specifically Christian shift in its range of implication, the essential contrast, up until the High Middle Ages, remained one between *natural* and *moral* and not *natural and supernatural.* The former distinction though, de Lubac argued, itself reflected the authentically Christian sense of the notion of the supernatural. For on the one hand there was created *nature;* on the other hand there was created *spirit,* which was free, and intellectually reflexive ('personal'). This 'moral' realm was in some sense not just created; it bore a more radical imprint of divinity: the *imago dei.*

In de Lubac's view, what undoubtedly upset the reign of the natural/moral *schema* was the irruption of Aristotelianism. Whereas neoplatonism itself in its own way explored a complex boundary between supernatural deity and material nature (in its schemes of emanations and returns, its doctrines of an innate belonging of the human soul to the upper astral reaches of the cosmos and beyond) and so had been readily Christianized by the Church fathers, Aristotelianism, even in its Arabic neoplatonized forms (because these were specifically philosophical, not theological), tended to insist that human nature could be adequately grasped as belonging to a natural cosmos, and with the help of a strictly analytic rather than intuitive reason. Even where rational contemplation passed over into an intuitive grasp of the unity of all, this remained a cosmic and unassisted vision, not a supernatural raising into identity with the first cause.

The question then becomes, was Aquinas able to assimilate the 'Arabic' Aristotle while retaining the older concepts of the supernatural? One of the problems with replying 'yes' to that, is that it might then seem that Aquinas continued to identify the 'supernatural' realm with the 'moral' realm. What then becomes of Aquinas's apparent discussion of merely 'natural' ethics after Aristotle? Whatever one's views on this problem, it is clear that de Lubac did, indeed, both for himself and Aquinas, insist that fully free and personal love for God and ethical response to the neighbor was only possible under the *aegis* of grace.[3] According to de Lubac, Aquinas distinguishes the latter kind of love and imperative from loves and imperatives that are merely 'natural', because natural affections grow out of our animal life, albeit articulated in a self-conscious way. Nevertheless he insists (following several crucial passages in Thomas) that even natural justice is impossible outside human governance by its ultimate supernatural end.

This is one example of the way, for de Lubac, the distinct Aristotelian moment in Aquinas remains subordinate to an Augustinianism blended with Procleanism (mediated by Dionysius and the Arabs). De Lubac explicitly endorses mid-century readings of Aquinas that stress the neoplatonic and Augustinian dimension, while at the same time his *Augustine* is much more humanist and 'Thomistic' than that of the previous run of French tradition.[4]

For the alternative, neo-scholastic construal of the "natural desire of the supernatural," however, Aquinas represented much more of a watershed and indeed the begin-

---

3. *Surnaturel*, p. 487. Here de Lubac shows that he thinks the older Augustinian natural/moral (in contrast to the natural/supernatural) distinction remains valid: "Ordre de la 'nature' et ordre de la 'moralité', ces deux ordres contiennent tous les conditions — les unes essentielles et nécessaires, les autres personnelles et libres."

4. See, for example, positive references to Geiger, Finance, and Fabro in *The Mystery of the Supernatural, Augustinianism and Modern Theology*, and *The Discovery of God*. Joseph Finance, whose *Être et Agir* is one of the most important modifications of Gilson's 'existential' reading of Aquinas in a more intellectualist and neoplatonic direction, was responsible for the first publication of the latter book in its original version — *De la Connaissance de Dieu* — during the period of de Lubac's ban from teaching and writing.

ning of proper scientific (as opposed to a semi-narrative and rhetorical) theology. For the first time, the neo-scholastics argued, it is clearly allowed by Aquinas and his contemporaries that there is an autonomous natural sphere comprising all of human activity outside the order of salvation. In this way, intrinsic human dignity and autonomy is allowed to emerge, while conversely and concomitantly the true gratuity of grace stands out along with the unnatural wonder of works of self-forgetting mercy inspired by our gracious elevation into friendship with God.

Put this way, it should be clear that, while 'neo-scholastic' suggests the fusty and obscurantist, this point of view — just because it is so modern and indeed the parent of modernity — runs far closer to average contemporary common sense than does the difficult (but palaeo-Christian) position of de Lubac. De Lubac's reading can seem simultaneously to compromise the legitimate domain of the secular *and* the contrasting surprisingness and gratuitousness of the divine works of freedom.

For de Lubac, though, neither humanist autonomy nor sheer external gratuity are desirable. In the first case, de Lubac noted (this is often overlooked in his work) that Cajetan and Suarez did not simply assert the independence and self-sufficiency of a natural *telos* over a supernatural one. To the contrary, where a teleological outlook remains in place — especially one reinforced by the neoplatonic sense that each level of being has a self-transcending outlook towards the next level, both above and below — it is likely that ultimate actual human orientation will be thought of as decisively influencing even the lowliest human proclivities. By contrast, the notion of a purely natural end only becomes plausible when the very idea of teleology has started to lose its sway. Hence in early modern scholasticism (partly under stoic influence) the 'natural' mode of being of a creature began to be thought of in terms not of its normative maximum flourishing, but its minimum self-sustainability, given the most fundamental (and non-teleological) facts about its mode of existence and operation.

Applied to humanity, this would allow a conception of individual and social self-sustaining in terms of the logic of survival and preservation of material well-being and freedom. The resultant set of norms can certainly be dubbed a desirable *telos,* but teleology is here secondary to a logic of self-regulation and self-sufficiency. It is *this* logic which for de Lubac permits a sense of *natura pura* to arise. And such autonomy is undesirable because, where the moral is cut off from religious practice and mystical self-loss, it is likely to result in joyless disciplinary programs for the maximizing of corporeal efficiency, and in the long run in nihilistic cults of individual and collective power.

This, for de Lubac, was (and is) the danger of pure humanism without a reference beyond humanity. On the other hand, this danger was ironically fostered by the illusory piety of a religion without humanity produced by the neo-scholastic understanding of grace. If grace now no longer fulfills the deepest longing of our nature, of our ethical, contemplative, and (even) naturally mystical impulses, then it resembles a politics proclaiming (rather like that advocated by Hannah Arendt) that it is puristically "about the political" and not (as she would say, "improperly") about education, welfare, transport, the environment and defense, etc. If grace does not elevate nature in such a way that it further develops the natural (as not sufficient unto itself), then just what *is* grace after all? It would seem to be something emptily *extrinsique,* to use de Lubac's word, itself explicitly borrowed by him from Aquinas's denial that grace is something *extraneum.*[5] Instead of grace being a participatory putting on of the divine nature (after the New Testament) it becomes a kind of purely nominal change in status by the decree of an arbitrary God mediated by the power structure of a church. Meanwhile, in the ethical sphere, supernatural charity now becomes something like "those acts of love which are performed with faith in God and therefore accorded merit," as opposed to the notion (the normative New Testament notion) that *wherever* love and mercy are shown, there divine charity is present. The specific mark of the supernatural in the latter case is nothing sheerly interior or ciphered, but rather the unlimited drive towards entire mutual reconciliation and peace for the whole creation. Just as one suspects that 'a purely political politics' will be only about power, so, likewise, a self-referential grace is all too likely to be the mask for mere worldly ecclesiastical dominion.

These sorts of arguments, and the genealogy that derives the secular from the *natura pura,* were expressed very powerfully by de Lubac.[6] Quite apart from the question of

5. *Summa contra gentiles* (hereafter SCG) 3.54(8). See also ST I-II. Q. 110, a1, where it is argued that *gratia ponat aliquid in anima.*

6. In addition to *Drama* and the books on the *Surnaturel,* see Henri de Lubac, *Theology in History* (San Francisco: Ignatius, 1996), pp. 223-367; and "Nature and Grace," in *The Word in History: The St. Xavier Symposium,* ed. T. Patrick Burke (London: Collins, 1968). In this speech, delivered on a tour to the U.S.A. in 1968,

the correct reading of Aquinas, it would be possible to argue that he is accurate in his understanding of the loss of the older Greek/Latin understanding of salvation and grace. It might be held that the attempt by Aquinas to incorporate Aristotle was simply a disaster. Why then did Aquinas matter for de Lubac? Why was de Lubac often indeed described within his order as a neo-Thomist, to distinguish him from the conservative neo-Suarezians?

The answer is, in part, that for de Lubac Aquinas represented the possibility of an East-West synthesis (Augustine plus the Dionysius/Damascene legacy) and even more crucially that the attempt to incorporate Aristotle *was* positive in so far as it meant a deeper reckoning with reflection upon the operations of nature and of this-worldly human behavior. Here again, de Lubac's 'paradoxical' doctrine of the supernatural cuts both ways at once. The older sense that *everything* must be viewed in an elevated light loses all cogency and depth if this light cannot ceaselessly shine within dark corners of finite existence newly explored. Without this continued deepening, the elevation would itself lapse back into the extrinsic.

For just this reason, de Lubac ceaselessly favored 'science' and theological dialogue with science. This is in part why he liked Origen: he admired his literal concern with place, time, season, and measurement. This is also why he later celebrated Cusa's and Bérulle's attempt spiritually to respond to the new heliocentric cosmology; it is finally

---

de Lubac traced the pervasive oscillation of American life between a sentimental piety on the one hand and a tasteless sensuality on the other, to the neoscholastic duality of nature and grace. His position on the United States here contrasts strongly with the uncritical enthusiasm of the later Maritain.

why he spent so much time reflecting, alongside Teilhard, on the import of evolutionary theory.

And it is for this reason that the compatibility of the patristic sense of the supernatural with the scholastic incorporation of Aristotle mattered for de Lubac. It is as if for him (and quite legitimately) Aquinas was an early Renaissance as much as he was a mediaeval figure: concerned to integrate into the Christian synthesis a new interest in nature and in urban civilization,

Given the centrality of this concern, though, the paucity of de Lubac's treatment of Aquinas on the supernatural and on grace seems surprising. In part it is explained by his knowledge of the work of Henri Bouillard and others who had already interpreted Aquinas's "natural desire of the supernatural" as an innate rather than an elicited desire in various studies.[7] Nevertheless, this *lacuna* in de Lubac's writings has long been exploited by his neo-scholastic critics.

Somewhat conflating de Lubac with Bouillard, one can summarize his view of Aquinas on the supernatural as follows. First of all, as noted, he sees that grace for Aquinas was not extrinsic, since it was not a *miracle*: as such it neither interrupted nor simply added to the order of nature; rather it intrinsically completed it.[8] Second, neither for angels nor men was there any stage of nature that might be qualified as impervious to sin, as incapable of this condition (as the neo-scholastics often thought, especially for angels) or, at the opposite extreme, *if* involved in sin, then to-

7. See note 1 above.

8. ST I-II. Q. 113, a10: justification is not normally a miracle and *naturaliter anima est gratiae capax*.

tally destroyed by it — as if to be 'natural' was equivalent with 'being sinless' (as later for Jansenius).[9] All of spiritual nature is permeated by *freedom,* and freedom as such is a relation to divine law and the ultimate divine end. Third, the natural desire of the supernatural in us cannot be merely elicited, because Aquinas says in the *Summa contra Gentiles* that we are drawn to the beatific vision in *exactly the same way* that every creature is moved by God towards some sort of unity with God. It is simply that we as *intellectual* creatures are moved in an intellectual way towards an intellectual union. The view of some commentators that, for Aquinas, the curiosity consequent upon natural wonder at created effects is purely epistemological can only be upheld if one ignores the foregoing sections of the relevant passages in which this statement is *ontologically* situated.[10] It is

9. For Aquinas, natural powers can be exercised either without sin or sinfully. Thus at ST I. Q. 83, a2 ad 3 he says that no *natural* liberty is removed by sin and at ST I-II. Q. 63, a1 that even in demons *bona naturalia manent.* For the question of angels, grace, sin, and beatitude in Aquinas see ST I. Q. 56, a3; Q. 62, aa1, 3, 6. For Aquinas angels were not created in a state of beatitude, but they *were* created in a state of grace — which Aquinas compares to a 'seed', and as with humans they can only be just and sinless under grace. See also Augustine, *Civitas Dei* IX 2: *"Simul eis [Angelis] et condens naturam et largiens gratiam."* See also René Mougel, "La Position de Jacques Maintain à L'égard de *surnaturel*: Le Péché de l'Ange, ou 'Esprit de Liberté'," in RT *Surnaturel,* pp. 73-98.

10. See, most decisively, SCG III. Q. 25. At [1] Aquinas says: "since all creatures, even those devoid of understanding, are ordered to God as to an ultimate end, all achieve this end to the extent that they participate somewhat in his likeness. Intellectual creatures attain it in a more special way, that is, through their proper operation in understanding Him. Hence, this must be the end of the intellectual creature, namely, to understand God."

That the desire to know God is an ontological *élan,* not a mere epistemological curiosity, is shown at [2]: "The ultimate end of each thing is God, as we have shown. So, each thing intends, as its ultimate end, to be united with God

clear from these passages that curiosity is but the spiritual manifestation of a general ontological drawing back to-

---

as closely as possible for it. Now, a thing is more closely united with God by the fact that it attains to His very substance in some manner, and this is accomplished when one knows something of the divine substance, rather than when one acquires some likeness of Him. Therefore an intellectual substance tends to divine knowledge as an ultimate end." At [5] Aquinas says that were the *telos* of the beatific vision *not* the end of spiritual creatures, they would have "a less noble end" than non-spiritual creatures who would still be united to God after their own fashion. (This shows that, in effect, given his justice, God could *not* have created purely natural spirit: proving de Lubac entirely right.) Unity "by assimilation" is contrasted with a higher unity "by cognition" at [6]. But at [8] it is stressed that the latter kind of unity "includes all other likenesses" — showing that the context for thinking about desire to know God here is a neoplatonic, exemplarist one. At [19] Aquinas says that anticipation of beatitude architectonically directs all other, lesser human modes of knowledge and desiring.

Only at [11] and [12] does Aquinas then speak more subjectively and epistemologically about our desire to know the cause of effects invoked by wonder.

Lawrence Feinberg, in his arch-reactionary book written to reinstate a Garrigou-Lagrange type position, *The Natural Desire to See God according to St. Thomas Aquinas and His Interpreters* (Rome: Apollinare Studi, 2001), cites only paragraphs 11-13 of this question on his pages 85-89. The ontological and neoplatonizing prelude is omitted from his discussion entirely! Frankly this selectivity gives the lie to the appearance of scholarly bulk and solidity which the weight of his tome seems to promise. Its exegetical method is much like that of the proof-texting of a Protestant fundamentalist.

This gets even more ludicrous when, in his discussion of ST I. Q. 12, a1 on his page 101, Feinberg begins his citation "Further, the same opinion [that no created intellect can see the essence of God] is against reason. For there resides in every man a natural desire to know the cause of any effect which he sees. . . ." Feinberg can easily argue that this is merely a movement of the will 'elicited' by detached cognitive curiosity because he has omitted the immediately preceding words which give the ontological context: "for the ultimate perfection of the rational creature is to be found in that which is the principle of its being, since a thing is perfect in so far as it attains to its principle."

Another passage in ST I-II. Q. 3, a8, which provides less of the ontological

wards God that is consequent upon the radical origin of all
things from God, such that they are nothing of themselves.

background for the natural desire to see God is deemed by Feinberg to be "the
most complete" treatment, presumably on the grounds that it gives a longer
version of the epistemological aspect that he is more comfortable with. . . . But
in fact, even the argument of this passage depends on the view that knowledge
of the divine essence is the ultimate *natural object* of the human intellect: "the
perfection of any power is determined by the nature of its object." Feinberg
simply ignores this statement of the ontology of the human intellect and fails
to discuss a further passage, ST I. Q. 8, a3 resp., where the relation of the intellect to its object is declared to be always a matter of a certain *presence* of this object (in this case God) in the intellect. Furthermore, it is made clear that this
mode of presence has (short of beatitude) grace as simply its intensest degree
— it is arguable that this passage is more radical than many of de Lubac's own
statements. It goes as follows: "God is said to be in a thing in two ways; in one
way after the manner of an efficient cause; and this He is in all things created
by Him; in another way He is in things as the object of operation is in the operator; and this is proper to the operations of the soul, according as the thing
known is in one who knows; and the thing desired in the one desiring. In this
way God is especially in the rational creature, which knows or loves Him actually or habitually. And because the rational creature possesses this prerogative
by grace. . . . He is said to be this in the saints by grace."

Note that knowing and desiring here keep pace with each other, whereas
for Feinberg and the neo-Thomist view there is *first* abstract intellectual curiosity (without desire) and *then* an elicited desiring (without any degree of knowledge).

At ST I-II. Q. 5, a5 ad 2, Aquinas deals with the seemingly resultant problem
that humanity, unlike lower creatures, is dependent on divine help in order to
reach his final end. But here he says, citing Aristotle, that achieving a more perfect good with assistance is still nobler than achieving a less perfect good on
one's own.

See in addition *De Veritate, Q.* 18, a1 ad 7: "*Homo factus erat ad videndum
Deum non in principio, sed in ultimo suae perfectionis.*"

Finally see also ST III. Q. 9, a3 for Aquinas's statement that the soul has an
aptitude for beatitude as being made in the *imago Dei.* The argument that the
latter is not a sort of static imprint but always, as in the Fathers, a dynamic pre-
science of grace, is an important aspect of de Lubac's argument.

In this neoplatonically assisted rendering of creation *ex nihilo* (where the neoplatonism is only invoked and deepened to do justice to this doctrine), beings only *exist* as longing in their own mode for God, and as expressing in their own mode their origin from God as ineluctably a tendency to return to God. Angels and humans do this consciously, cognitively and willingly. Hence *as spirits* they are innately called to the beatific vision. The curiosity instigated by created effects is itself an erotic curiosity; while inversely the 'elicited' desire to know God is itself a cognitive desire. There is (one can add to de Lubac) no Scotist-influenced duality of will and intellect present in Aquinas as there is later in Cajetan and Suarez. De Lubac himself always insisted that the 'will' in humanity was no mere faculty, but an integral expression of personhood itself: will, intellect, and feeling.[11]

According to Aquinas's conception of spirit, God is in the soul as the object of an (ontological) operation is in the operator.[12] The natural orientation to the supernatural therefore indicates the presence of the divine to us always in the depths: our latent mystical condition. This is so proper to our nature that de Lubac asked, in the fourth place: why, if grace is a kind of superadded extra and there can be nature without sin (according to the neo-scholastics' argument), should a knowing refusal of grace, for the en-

---

11. Henri de Lubac, *Pic de la Mirandole* (Paris: Aubier-Montaigne, 1974), 171. De Lubac says here, admiringly, that for Pico freedom was "the deep substance of humanity" rather than a faculty and that his radical sense of human liberty was in no way akin to that of late scholastic voluntarism.

12. ST I. Q. 8, a3 resp. See the citation and discussion of this passage in n. 9 above.

tire tradition, incur the *poena damni* for human nature as such?

In the fifth and final place, de Lubac argued that, for Aquinas, the natural desire for the supernatural could not, in divine justice, be disappointed, without violating the Aristotelian principle that a natural impulse to an end cannot (unless abnormally) be frustrated: *Desiderium naturale nequit esse inane.* Neo-Thomist arguments to the effect that this ignores merely intentional and instrumental pursuits of ends are not to the point if — as has been seen — there is here an ontological drive to the final end.[13] No mere quest of the mind, or search for whatever will enable a vague, naturally-known about happiness, is invoked by Aquinas.

De Lubac nevertheless knew that application of this axiom (that a natural impulse cannot be frustrated) to grace violated another Aristotelian axiom to the effect that every authentically natural movement towards an end must be capable of realization out of its own resources. This was the principle appealed to by Cajetan in the name of a purer Aristotelianism and a more immanent ontology, where one does not have to explain the essences of this world ultimately in terms of the lure of the ineffable. I have dubbed such a refused position, which always refers the 'beingness' of finite being to transcendent *esse,* a 'non-ontology.' Later I shall show how approaches to this sort of 'non-ontology' in neoplatonism, which violate the second Aristotelian axiom invoked by Cajetan, are appealed to by Aquinas to support his account of the working of the supernatural at a

13. See, for example, Feinberg, *The Natural Desire to See God,* pp. 525ff.

level *even below* that of the creator-created relationship. This confirms further what is already apparent in de Lubac: namely that his account of grace and the supernatural is *ontologically revisionary*. The natural desire cannot be frustrated, yet it cannot be of itself fulfilled. Human nature in its self-exceeding seems in justice to require a gift — yet the gift of grace remains beyond all justice and all requirement. This paradox is for de Lubac only to be entertained because one must remember that the just requirement for the gift in humanity is itself a created gift.

Cajetan and neo-scholasticism, by contrast, leave philosophical ontology alone in its immanence: the being of human nature, as of everything else, can be specified without reference to God, or only to God as ultimate efficient cause. On the other hand, cosmic and human being in no way (as it does for de Lubac) anticipates grace. The structures of grace are without precedent: yet in practice neo-scholasticism will have to speak of them in terms of analogues taken from an immanent univocal ontology. Since nothing in 'purely natural' being of itself participates in divine *esse* or by analogical ascent negates its own non-self-sufficiency, these analogues will be purely in terms of a 'quantitative' extension of the range of an adequately 'given' meaning. And what natural analogues to grace will be available in these terms save those of an anonymous and overwhelming force? Or a nominal and invisible raising of status which yet commands a visible jurisdiction?

So while de Lubac linked the loss of the true account of the supernatural to the loss of teleology, he also linked it to the rise of a univocal ontology and a merely semantic account of analogy sundered from a metaphysic of existential participation, which could at times be combined with an overly formal *via negativa* refusing a doctrine of eminence (the view that a positive term like 'good', negated of God in its finite significance, is nonetheless affirmed of him in a replete significance of goodness only remotely accessible by us). De Lubac insisted that analogy concerned the range of *judgment* of a soul participating in divine spirit, not simply the range in meaning of a linguistic concept.[14] Reference to debates concerning analogy is not accidental. In his book on Barth, von Balthasar brought together de Lubac's account of the supernatural with Erich Przywara's restoration of the *analogia entis* to refute both a liberal theology starting from a human foundation below, and a Barthian commencement with a revelation over against a nature at once utterly depraved and merely passively open to the divine (in the sense of a passivity 'opposed' to human activity, not a radical passivity with respect to God in the heart of the active itself).[15] These two refutations imply a 'suspended middle' and a non-ontology, since Przywara's analogy and de Lubac's supernatural be-

14. De Lubac, *The Discovery of God*, trans. Alexander Dru (New York: P. J. Kennedy, 1960), pp. 200-201. De Lubac says here that such a merely semantic concept of analogy — ignoring the participation of *esse* and *intelligere* — must retain an element of univocity (since here 'meaning' is thought of as something basically within our capacity for apprehension, or else as exceeding it only in a *sheerly* negative way, not as an 'eminence' into which we have some mysterious degree of insight).

15. Hans Urs von Balthasar, *The Theology of Karl Barth*, trans. John Drury (New York: Holt, Rinehart, and Winston, 1971). I do not mean here *analogia entis* in the ontotheological sense of an analogy between God and creatures 'within being,' but in Aquinas's sense of an unmediated analogy between finite being and God as himself the plenitude of *esse*.

long neither to natural theology nor to doctrine, while at the same time they belong to both and encompass both. Natural analogies for God remotely anticipate even the divine essence, while the discourse of grace must perforce still deploy names that initially refer to the created order.

Nevertheless, considerable obscurities remain. Is the natural desire for the supernatural *already* the working of grace? In that case, why is it a natural desire? But if it is not already grace at work, is there not an *exigency* for grace on the part of human nature, which suggests that it unfolds as if from a seed, rather than arriving from without? And if the cosmos returns to God more fully through spirits, did God *have* to create spirits? Is it truly inevitable that the latter are orientated to the beatific vision, given the continuity of intellect with the function of the animal soul, according to Aristotle? Finally, if the orientation to grace is simply the mode taken by createdness in the intellectual creature, what becomes of the distinction between the *datum optimum* of creation on the one hand, and the *donum perfectum* of grace on the other?

All these questions continued to haunt de Lubac long after he had seen the back of the Gestapo and the secular power of his Catholic Rightist opponents.

⳺ 3 ⳺

Around Humani Generis

Although we have seen that de Lubac was as much an
'Origenist' or a 'Thomist' as an 'Augustinian', he has been
regarded by various neo-Thomists as perpetuating the classical theses of Baius and Jansenius. Both Baius and Jansenius in various ways and in various degrees denied the
existence of a 'pure nature' in spiritual existence; to repeat
this Jansenist position, for de Lubac's critics, was to repeat
also their semi-Calvinist denigration of the natural sphere.
Hence when de Lubac was not being accused of 'naturaliz-
ing the supernatural' by a form of *a priori* argument based
upon the structures of the human spirit, he was being accused of entirely evacuating the natural sphere in favor of
the rule of grace.

In point of fact though, de Lubac sought to do neither.
If he was attacking a reading of Aquinas which elided his
fundamental Augustinianism, he was equally attacking the
Jansenist, non-humanist version of Augustine. Already in
Surnaturel, and then further in *Augustinisme et théologie
moderne,* he provided a reading of Baius and Jansenius

which showed how their refusal of pure nature, far from advocating a genuine natural desire for the supernatural, was really complicit with Cajetan's *acceptance* of pure nature.[1] Indeed, as de Lubac demonstrates, they took the latter process further, in so far as they could no longer see why the sinless Adam in Eden stood under any need for grace at all. This, for de Lubac, is the point where finally grace in the West ceases in any sense to be deification, because it no longer has to do fundamentally with a gratuitous raising of humanity above itself to God but is now merely a judicial corrective for sin. (By contrast there are traces of deification even in Erasmus, Luther, and Calvin.) The 'grace' that for Baius is provided for Adam prior to the Fall, is merely the reward due to the merit of his perfect pure nature. But this absolute pre-lapsarian naturalistic optimism actually entails its post-lapsarian 'Calvinist' obverse: after sin, an essentially self-sufficient pure nature is totally destroyed (or almost so for Jansenius) and becomes utterly dependent for any benefit upon an extrinsic divine decree. Here a religion without humanism still correlates with a humanism without religion, but the dialectical collusion has been dynamized around the event of the Fall.

Nothing illustrates more clearly de Lubac's assault upon opposites which are really two halves of one distorted picture: autonomous nature, external grace.

Nevertheless, it did not seem completely clear how de Lubac was himself to avoid dissolving his aporetic paradox

---

1. *Surnaturel* (Paris: Desclée de Brouwer, 1991), pp. 15-187; *Augustinianism and Modern Theology,* trans. Lancelot Sheppard (New York: Herder & Herder, 1969), pp. 1-118.

either into the first — a kind of Kantianism which would naturalize and rationalize grace; or else into the second — a new mode of Jansenism.

The second danger appeared especially to loom if the ordering to the supernatural is itself the work of grace, historically mediated: in that case the post-Eden restoration is to correct an utter devastation, a nature destroyed, which is inconsistent with a Catholic (and Christian) sense that Creation, insofar as it remains in being at all, persists in some degree of goodness. Moreover, this interpretation of the ordering of the supernatural, as we saw, is one aspect (but one aspect only, since here balanced by a notion of a natural 'potential of obedience' for grace which prevents any possibility of a natural total depravity) of Cajetan's interpretation of Aquinas's 'natural desire for the supernatural'. (This 'historicism' on Cajetan's part can validly be read as a 'Christian humanist' aspect of his work, despite his opening up also of a sheerly secular humanist terrain.) In *The Mystery of the Supernatural* such a perspective is more explicitly refused by de Lubac, who indeed goes so far as to say that the natural desire for God in no way whatsoever anticipates grace.[2] Yet if this natural desire is not a mere

2. *The Mystery of the Supernatural,* trans. Rosemary Sheed (London: Herder & Herder, 1967), pp. 110-11, 41: "'The fact that the nature of spiritual being, as it actually exists, is not conceived of as an order destined to close in finally upon itself, but is in a sense open to an inevitably supernatural end, does not mean that it already has in itself, or as part of its basis, the smallest positively supernatural element. It does not mean that this nature 'as nature, and by nature' is elevated.'" But this could almost be neo-Thomistic and elsewhere de Lubac asserts that the natural desire for the supernatural is present by virtue of the supernatural even if one does not call this "grace" (and this scruple is logical if one is talking about the *hinge* between grace and nature). See, for example, his

'means' to the beatific vision (and de Lubac at least once unfortunately describes it this way, even though this seems at variance with the general thrust of his thought), then this 'non-anticipation' seems inconsistent with a substantively 'absolute' desire for beatitude (which is absolute because not contingent upon the historical divine call to salvation), since this absoluteness implies some lure on the part of beatitude itself — which could only be realized as a kind of foretaste of grace. De Lubac had earlier in *Surnaturel* said that the natural desire for the supernatural is "something" of God, though it is not yet grace.[3] But in deference to *Humani Generis,* de Lubac now *drops* from his re-worked "The Mystery of the Supernatural" article the idea that there is a positive advance manifestation of the supernatural that "gives the natural desire for the supernatural" — even though this notion of an inchoate presence of the ultimate supernatural object of human knowledge *always* to the human knower is clearly affirmed by Aquinas (see Chapter 2, note 10 above). *Now* the "longing" of the

---

article "The Mystery of the Supernatural" in *Theology in History* (San Francisco: Ignatius, 1996), p. 303: "it is not in any case nature that of itself calls the supernatural, it is the supernatural, if one can say so, that arouses nature before summoning it to receive it [the supernatural]." Or again, p. 313: "The desire for the supernatural, as natural and serious as it may be, is not in any case what determines the effective gift of it on God's part. Between these two terms, the relation can only be inverse: it is the will of the donor that awakens the desire in the one that it wants to reach."

3. On grace as only means see *Surnaturel,* p. 393. On anticipation of the supernatural within the natural see *Surnaturel,* p. 487: [speaking of the natural desire for the supernatural] *"quoi qu'il y ait de bonnes raisons de l'appeler 'naturel' (puisqui'il est essentiellement dans la nature et qu'il en exprime du fond) on doit ajouter qu'il est déja en un sens, quelque chose de Dieu."*

soul is said to be "born of a lack" and not to involve any "participation" in supernatural being "even initially or distantly." (Yet contradictorily de Lubac still speaks of an always present divine "call" that generates the natural desire for the supernatural and of an *absolute,* not *conditional,* will of human nature towards the beatific vision; "absolute" here includes the idea that it cannot be frustrated without causing abysmal spiritual distress.) Scotus is cited as saying that man is *indispositus* to his end, and indeed this interpretation of the desire as a mere negative lack is in keeping with the Scotist and even the Jansenist reading of Augustine. De Lubac cites the latter as speaking of man as left after the fall with the *imago Dei* but not the 'participation' that grace alone can give. But again this depends upon a Scotistic rendering of Augustine (actually refused by de Lubac elsewhere) which reads the *imago Dei* as the univocal presence of the image of the Trinity in us as memory, mind, and will. For Augustine himself, by contrast, the *imago Dei* that always remains involves some degree of participation in the Godhead, if not the participation of grace, and it is destined to rise, by grace, into a *similitudo* of God.

It follows that de Lubac's concessions to the Church hierarchy here seem to shift him more to a Scotist (and even latently Jansenist) exposition of his theory — which makes the natural desire for the supernatural not any longer participatory, but only vaguely aspirational, and in consequence more voluntaristic than intellectualist (since in the latter case the desire would receive in advance some sort of 'stamp' of what it sought — as indeed is the case for Aquinas). But is de Lubac consistent? Or does he even really mean this? In this book he also cites Bérulle, speaking of "a movement so deep and powerful that the will cannot fight against it" — hardly a matter of mere lack or negative desire.

This is not to disagree with de Lubac that the natural desire for the supernatural is not an immanent 'seed' of grace. No, such desire is the gift of the anticipation of gift (as de Lubac earlier knew). But if this natural desire is already a gift from above, then *just for this reason* its sense of lack is aroused by some remote foretaste of presence. As we shall later see, it is by no means clear from his later writings that de Lubac really abandoned his earlier position.[4]

On the other hand, de Lubac's denial in *The Mystery of the Supernatural* that the natural desire for the supernatural

---

4. *The Mystery of the Supernatural*, pp. 109-12. For a comparison with the earlier tone of the article entitled "The Mystery of the Supernatural" see note 2 above. These contrasts (despite the statement concerning the abstract possibility of a 'pure nature' in the essay) give the lie to the view that de Lubac was not obliged to put things differently by the encyclical. Textual appearances force one to disagree here with Georges Chantraine, S.J., in his article "Le surnaturel, discernement de la pensée Catholique de H. de Lubac," in RT *Surnaturel*, pp. 31-51. For de Lubac's continued invocation of the divine *appelée*, see *Mystery of the Supernatural*, pp. 70 and 98; for continued talk of an "absolute" desire, see p. 235; for the citation of Bérulle see p. 74. More of the citation is as follows: "And it is a movement so deep and powerful that the will cannot affect it except to fight against it; that no sin we commit can hold it back; that hell itself cannot obliterate it. That movement will last as long as the creature itself, and is inseparable from it. And the struggle that will take place in hell between the movement naturally imprinted upon the creature by the Creator, and the movement of will whereby the creature turns away from him, will be one of the chief and everlasting torments of the damned." This Thomistic intellectualism is at variance with the Scotistic moment farther on in the book. The later presentation of Bérulle, Pico, and Cusa in *Pic de la Mirandole* might lead one to believe that the Bérullean view is the deeper de Lubac. How far was he aware of this contradiction? For Scotus's understanding of the image of the Trinity in man, see Olivier Boulnois, *Être et Représentation* (Paris, PUF, 1999), pp. 107-14.

is as yet grace itself, is not really a 'concession' in relation to his original views. On the contrary, it is necessary to sustain them, for if this desire is already grace then there is nothing in human nature of itself — prior to all culture and history, even if one allows that this human nature is a cultural nature — which urges towards the beatific vision. Then one is back with extrinsicism. On the other hand, if pure nature of itself *demands* not merely the possibility but the actuality of the beatific vision, then grace cannot be a gift. To sustain his "suspended middle" de Lubac (when he is being coherent) strives rather to say that while Creation is the gift of independent existence and grace is the irresistible gift of nonetheless free and deified existence (joining the creature to the Creator as regards intellect, will, and personhood if not essential being), then the natural desire of the supernatural is the gift of the bond between the two, negotiated by the spirit's freedom. If Creation implies both autonomous being and entirely heteronomous gift, while grace implies a raising of oneself *as* oneself to the *beyond* oneself, then the natural desire of the supernatural implies the dynamic link between the two orders that constitutes spirit, such that this link is at once entirely an aspect of the Creation and entirely also the work, in advance of itself, of grace which unites human creatures to the Creator. The link between the gift of Creation and the gift of deification — which is angelic or human existence in its defining *acme* — must also be a gift of something at once wholly divine and wholly human. It follows that the natural desire for the supernatural cannot ever remain only a part of nature, yet cannot ever yet really be grace — rather like the problematic plane between two and three dimensions in fractal geometry. Yet in another sense — since there can be no third term here, as de Lubac insists against Rahner, amongst others, just as there is no actual fractal plane between the normal dimensions — it must still be entirely nature and must already be entirely grace. De Lubac never stated quite this extremity of paradox all at once; yet at various times he made diverse statements which imply just this complex entanglement.

De Lubac thus had to clarify, at one end of his problematic, the relation between the natural desire for the supernatural and the actual historical offer of grace (even if he took this, with the tradition, as always already begun immediately after the Fall and as mediated to all humans by typological anticipation).[5] But at the other end, he also had to clarify the issues of *natura pura*. As we have seen from the quotation in the introduction, *Humani Generis* challenged him to explain whether or not there could really be *no* spiritual existence outside the destiny of supernatural beatitude. Already, in the essay "The Mystery of the Supernatural," written before the encyclical (but perhaps anticipating that it was imminent), de Lubac conceded (or alternatively made explicit): first, that in theory God could have created a cosmos without spiritual creatures; second, that he could have created spiritual creatures without a natural orientation to the supernatural; and, finally, that the latter in no way obligates grace.[6]

---

5. *Catholicism*, trans. Lancelot Sheppard (London: Burns and Oates, 1937), p. 194: unbelievers "will be able . . . to obtain . . . salvation by virtue of the mysterious bonds that unite them to believers." See also, John Milbank and Catherine Pickstock, *Truth in Aquinas* (London: Routledge, 2001), p. 39.

6. "The Mystery of the Supernatural," pp. 299-316; *The Mystery of the Supernatural*, pp. 104-7.

However, on this last point we have already seen that de Lubac cannot really keep some sort of anticipation of grace at bay from the natural orientation to the supernatural. A kind of sadistic withholding of the fullness of what has already been to a degree imparted might be formally conceivable under the aegis of the *potentia Dei absoluta,* but it would not be compatible with the eternal nature of a God who freely loves.

A parallel consideration then applies to the second point: the counterfactual possibility of spiritual creatures not destined to see God may be barely granted in order to secure the divine freedom, yet the actual existence of creatures destined to see God is itself the disclosure of the limitless nature of the divine self-sharing. This alone reveals God to be supernatural charity — which is his very essence: coincident indeed with his divine freedom, but not something that he could choose not to have, as if this would render him more free.

Moreover, de Lubac insists that the counterfactually imagined purely natural spirits would be unimaginably other than actually existent angels or humans: they would simply be a different genus altogether from spirits as we know them. Here de Lubac strongly parted company with the neo-scholastic legacy for which pure nature was perfectly conceivable. For this tradition, human beings without grace would be more or less the human beings that we are familiar with — living in families and cities under laws and customs and exercising modes of natural religion. But this view tends to suggest that the difference that grace makes is something like the visibility of institutional Christianity plus the *sheerly* invisible effects of grace in people's souls. Against this literally incredible cultic banalization of an ancient tradition, de Lubac suggests, instead, that without the lure of grace there would be no self-exceeding *élan* that generates the diversity and restlessness of human culture. Yet the nature of this lure is only fully shown in Christ. Hence the difference that grace makes is something more like the infinite (practical and theoretical) task of *re-reading* all of human reality in the light of grace — the task proper to a diffuse corporate body, rather than a task committed to a juridical institution.

However, it is clear (despite all-around evasion of the point) that *Humani Generis* indeed *did* entertain the notion of identifiable pure nature. For its claim is that only the supposition of the possibility of the creation of purely natural spirits preserves the gratuity of grace — as opposed to what belongs intrinsically to human nature. For de Lubac the supposition was weakly regulative in the sense that it guarantees that God is not by alien necessity the God of grace. But for Pius XII it was more strongly regulative in that it serves to distinguish God's gracious action from his creative action. Grace is gratuitous because it gives to us what by no means belongs to us by nature — nature here including such things as the capacity to walk, the power of speech, and the tendency to political organization, which we can readily identify as innate and universal.

In both the essay and the book versions of "The Mystery of the Supernatural," however, de Lubac denies that the thesis of pure nature can guarantee the gratuity of grace. In the original essay (which is superior), in one of the most crucial passages in de Lubac's entire *oeuvre*, he deals with this point in terms of the logic of the *gift*, relating it directly to the Heideggerean-Gilsonian question of the logic of *existence*.[7]

The neo-Thomists, de Lubac implies, think in terms of God and creatures as individual beings on the same plane, either competitively jostling with each other or forming compacts to specify respective spheres of influence. They forget (as Gilson has now reminded them) that God is *esse* itself, not an *ens* but the eminent reality of all *entia*.[8] As such he never, properly speaking, interacts with creatures. But this fact has implications for the logic of the gift. We imagine that the gratuitous needs to be contrasted with the obligatory or the inherent; yet this only applies to the inter-actions between beings in the ontic realm. In the realm of the ontological difference, of the creative emergence of *entia* from *esse*, gratuity arises before necessity or obliga-tion and does not even require this contrast in order to be comprehensible. The creature as creature is not the recipi-ent of a gift; it *is* itself this gift. The same consideration ap-plies to a spiritual creature: as spirit he does not receive a gift; he is this gift of spirit. Later, in *Pic de la Mirandole*, de Lubac expands this argument in terms of theses derived from Nicholas of Cusa and Pierre Bérulle and picked up again in the twentieth century by Laberthonnière and, more recently, Claude Bruaire: since there is no preceding recipient, the spirit is a gift to a gift and the gift of giving oneself to oneself, which is the only way consciously to *live being a gift* and so to be spirit. This reflexivity of giving is for

7. "The Mystery of the Supernatural," pp. 218-99.
8. See Etienne Gilson, *Letters to Henri de Lubac* (San Francisco: Ignatius, 1986), *passim*.

Cusa the mark of spirit, while every *ens* as *ens* also gives itself *(se dat)* according to a specific contraction, and all beings reciprocally exchange natures and even 'names' with each other.[9]

To receive spirit, according to de Lubac, is always to be conscious of partial reception: one knows that one is not all of possible knowing and willing and feeling and moreover that, since our share of these things *is* what we are, we do not really command them, after the mode of a recipient of possessions. Hence to will, know, and feel is to render gratitude, else we would refuse ourselves as constituted as gift. Such gratitude to an implied infinite source can only be, as gratitude, openness to an unlimited reception from this source which is tantamount to a desire to know the giver. In this way, for de Lubac, the opening to the question of being of the intellectual creature (what Heidegger called *Dasein*) is at the same time the gratitude of spirit to the unknown giver, the desire further to understand this giver and thereby to comprehend and receive better his mysterious gift. In *Les chemins de Dieu*, de Lubac summed up his linking of the Gilsonian problematic of *esse* with his own problematic of the *surnaturel* (or of *espirit*) as follows: "intelligence is the faculty of being because spirit is the genuine capacity for God."[10]

Hence for de Lubac — and those who have elaborated him on this point, especially Claude Bruaire — the logic of

9. *Pic de la Mirandole* (Paris: Aubier-Montaigne, 1974), pp. 334-35, 340; Claude Bruaire, *L'Être et L'Esprit* (Paris: PUF, 1983), esp. pp. 9-87. Nicholas of Cusa, *De Visione Dei* 7; *De Dato Patris Lumnium* 2; Pierre Bérulle, *Opuscula* 32, 33.

10. *The Discovery of God,* trans. Alexander Dru (New York: P. J. Kennedy, 1960), p. 75.

spirit as gift governs both the realm of nature and the realm of grace and the hinge between them that is the mystery of the supernatural. Were one to allow the thesis of pure nature, says de Lubac, no gratuity of grace would thereby be established, but only the kind of gratuity proper to a this-worldly ontic gift offered to an already present and 'ungiven' recipient. This model cannot reach radical divine ontological gratuity, for two reasons.

First of all (this is elaborated by de Lubac elsewhere) one still faces the sort of problems which plagued all theologians after Scotus and especially those of the seventeenth century: namely, how does the pure nature receive the gift — of its own volition or by the gift as standing over against its natural ungivenness? The first solution is Pelagian; the second, in Lutheran fashion, sees grace as overriding our freedom. Secondly (as de Lubac states here), since all concede that actual concrete humanity *is* elevated to grace, how can the latter remain gratuitous *within* this elevation and not just in relation to the postulated moment prior to such elevation? Grace, like the act of creation, presupposes *nothing* — not even Creation (since God *could* have made an immediately beatified angel); hence it cannot be gratuitous in relation to a contrasting necessity or a recipient existing independently of its reception.

It follows that where grace is thought of as an extrinsic superaddition and as *requiring* the contrasting notion of the non-grace of pure nature, then it is covertly subordinated to an idolatrous and impossible common medium between nature and grace, just as God thought of as a mere *ens* is covertly subordinated to a univocal *esse* shared between him and creatures.

This 'common medium' would have to be something like a negotiated *concursus* between divine and human wills, as if they really operated on the same plane. Grace on this model will either depend (as with Baius and Jansenius) on our agreement to receive it, or else it will coerce our wills entirely. And if nature and grace are here spatially *outside each other* (on an extrinsicist model) then this situation will pertain not just at the moment of reception of grace, but throughout the experience of salvation. *Either* we will independently contribute to the reception and meriting of grace ('Pelagianism') and in that case it will be something chosen or deserved and not a gift, *or else* it will be something that externally compels our will and, again, no more a gift than is a brick wall that we might inadvertently run into. Whereas the gift of grace involves a change in status of the spirit itself, ontic models of the contrast of gift with non-gift dissolve such radical gratuity altogether.

In this way (here elaborated) de Lubac turned the tables on his opponents. The supposition of an actual identifiable pure nature in fact ruins the articulation of divine gratuity and can historically be shown to have done so. The gift of deification is guaranteed by *no* contrast, not even with Creation, never mind nature. How could it be, since like the Creation, it is a gift to a gift which, in this spiritual instance, the gift then gives to itself in order to sustain its only nature? How could it be guaranteed by contrast, since the gift of deification is so much in excess of Creation that it entirely includes it? In the ultimate experience of the supernatural which orients it, namely the beatific vision, our entire being is transfigured by the divine light. Here we *become* the reception of this light and there is no longer any additional 'natural' recipient of this reception. But this ensures, and does not destroy, radical gratuity. This is perhaps the subtle heart of de Lubac's theology. In these *loci*, de Lubac inaugurated a new discourse of the spirit as gift which he may well have seen as more satisfactory than the older language of the supernatural (he at least once indicated that this could not really do justice to the paradox of grace).[11] This discourse, if it deals with the middle that is suspended between nature and grace, does not itself belong either to philosophy or theology (as Bruaire's work tends to show). Accordingly, de Lubac stated in *The Mystery of the Supernatural* that the natural desire for the supernatural could itself, though 'natural', only fully be recognized by faith and not by reason alone.[12]

---

11. Henri de Lubac, *Atheisme et Sens de L'Homme* (Paris: Aubier-Montaigne, 1968), p. 95; Hans Urs von Balthasar, *The Theology of Henri de Lubac: An Overview* (San Francisco: Ignatius, 1991), p. 68.

12. *The Mystery of the Supernatural*, pp. 274-75.

❧ 4 ❧

Supernatural, Spirit, and Cosmos

By contrast with the revisions of *Surnaturel* (published as *Augustinisme et Théologie Moderne* and *Le Mystère du Surnaturel*) after *Humani Generis*, two other later writings of de Lubac suggest a continued effort to deepen the uncompromising radicalism of his initial thesis. These are his posthumously published fragment "Tripartite Anthropology," which sketches part of the projected book on mysticism, and his late work assaulting Renaissance scholarship, *Pic de la Mirandole.*

In "Tripartite Anthropology" it becomes yet clearer that the thesis regarding the supernatural involves ontological revision.[1] Here de Lubac argues, against many other scholars, that St. Paul's division between body, soul, and spirit reflects Hebrew rather than Greek anthropology and was

---

1. Henri de Lubac, "Tripartite Anthropology" in *Theology in History* (San Francisco: Ignatius, 1996), pp. 117-233. See also Maximus the Confessor, *Ambiguum* 7:"On the beginning and end of Rational creatures," in *On the Cosmic Mystery of Jesus Christ,* trans. P. M. Blowers and R. L. Wilken (New York: St. Vladimir Press, 2003), pp. 45-75.

48

first introduced to classical antiquity by Philo. (He also notably seeks to demonstrate that Erasmus, who accepted the division, was more authentically Pauline than Luther, who later abandoned it for a doctrine of post-lapsarian total depravity.) This repartition was, for de Lubac, supremely developed by Origen and echoes throughout the Christian mystical tradition. Already in Paul, whereas the contrast of soul is body, the contrast of *pneuma* is *sarx*, the flesh. This "flesh" is the false egoism and claim to autonomy of the person; inversely *pneuma* exceeds the psychic, because it is what underlies the entire person as the point of his derivation from God. For Maximus the Confessor *pneuma* is the mode taken in us by the *logoi* that underlie every creature, diversely displaying the one divine *Logos* in which they are ingathered. It is Augustine's unthinkable interior spark, where we are more ourselves in being God and where God as God in his ("impossible") omnipresence is most radically and kenotically exteriorized. For here he shares (as far as ontologically possible) his full essence in its aspect of intellection, which is yet more fundamental than *esse*, since if *esse* is through and through intellectual, *esse* as such must be *intelligere*, for it should be defined by its highest aspect, if this is all-permeating. We know from our own experience that intellect is a kind of being that in a way can 'be' all things (as Aristotle said). Hence if we ought to say that God as *esse* must be throughout intellect, we possess in ourselves some clue as to why *esse* as such is intellectual.

Here de Lubac echoes Rousselot's intellectualism as superior to Gilson's existentialism, although for him intelligence and will are radically fused and often he deploys "will" to stand for the whole spiritual nature, while explicitly repudiating any implications of (scholastic) voluntarism. He implies that a metaphysics of spirit is at least co-original with a metaphysics of being. This is highly consonant with Eckhart, and de Lubac reads the latter's extreme statements of identity between God and the human soul in terms of the Origenist *longue durée*. Spiritual beings in their deepest identity are lured to unity with God — even in some sense already possess this unity. For Origen and other Church fathers, as de Lubac noted, the *pneuma* can never suffer damnation, even when the rest of the person is condemned — rendering this condition perhaps a temporary one. It is hard to resist the conclusion that for de Lubac the desire for the supernatural *is* spirit, and spirit is the desire for the supernatural. The non-publication and unfinished character of "Tripartite Anthropology" is perhaps politically significant.

In *Pic de la Mirandole,* by contrast, de Lubac rarely expresses his own theological views.[2] On the other hand, his apparent endorsement of the fundamental positions of Pico, Cusa, and Bérulle surely speaks volumes. More perhaps than any other book written to date by any hand, this book seeks to demolish the myth of the Renaissance. Certainly, de Lubac concedes, after the late-scholastic dissolution of the synthesis between technical and mystical theology, there ensued a spiritual hunger which some sought to sate by fascinated importation from Byzantium of the revived pagan Academy of Gemistus Plethon, later semi-Christianized by Ficino. On the other hand, other equally important 'Renaissance' currents were not in search of a

---

2. *Pic de la Mirandole* (Paris: Aubier-Montaigne, 1974), *passim.*

purely natural religion. To the contrary, on de Lubac's reading, Pico della Mirandola and Nicholas of Cusa deliberately *rejected* the 'pure nature' that had begun to emerge from late scholasticism. Concomitantly it was Pico, not the purveyors of scholastic tradition, who grasped the ontological difference in Aquinas; in *De Ente et Uno* he pitted the Thomistic doctrine that *esse* is the highest (though it is also *unum*) against the newly revived pagan neoplatonic view that a necessarily impersonal and non-intellectual 'One' stands above 'Being'.[3]

For Pico, this metaphysics was ultimately theological and if he (like Cusa) more radically collapsed together philosophical and theological discourses than did Aquinas, then this for de Lubac is a sign not of a burgeoning humanist naturalism but rather of a return to the patristic understanding of philosophy as 'Christian' and an adoption of a more radical barrier against a 'pure nature' which is the actual — scholastic! — source of a debased autonomous humanism.

In Pico, de Lubac discovered further dimensions of *pneuma,* or of the natural desire for the supernatural, that are specific to *humans* rather than to angels. Strictly following Philo and the Fathers, especially the Greek Fathers, Pico stressed that man is a *Proteus,* alone not pronounced 'good' after his creation in Genesis by God, because his goodness was dependent upon the free choice of his will (even though *as* free it naturally chooses the good). Man has nothing specific about him, he is compounded of the mineral, vegetable, animal and 'angelic' (spiritual) and can

---

3. *Pic de la Mirandole,* pp. 261-87.

abase himself to the earth or raise himself to the stars. (For Cusa, likewise, man is equally *humanus mundus* and *humanus Deus*.) He is like a table that builds itself, a painting that paints itself. (Bérulle later echoed all this.)[4]

So here the inward mystical tension of the *capax Dei* is shown (following the Fathers) also to be an external cosmic and cultural tension. As in itself 'nothing', the entire Creation aspires to return to God and to acknowledge God and can only fully do so in Man the Microcosm. In apparently endorsing this thematic (as he did also in the case of Teilhard de Chardin's theories), de Lubac seems to say (despite occasional denials) that the cosmos is unimaginable without Humanity, which holds all of creation together. In addition he appears to say that creation *as such* involves grace, since it is, in the first place, the entire *cosmos* that has a natural desire for God, while spiritual existence, especially human existence, is the *upshot* of this circumstance. How can this stand then, with de Lubac's denial that grace is a mere *sequela creationis?* Simply by recalling de Lubac's exposition of radical gift. Deification is not there because of creation; rather creation is there because of deification, as the apex and microcosmic summation of created glory. This parallels the trumping of *esse* by *intellegere*, being by spirit.

One begins to see now the components of de Lubac's half-concealed, more radical version of the supernatural.

---

4. *Pic de la Mirandole*, pp. 114-231; 327-52. See also George Herbert's poem "The Pulley" (cited by Blowers and Wilken in their frontispiece to Maximus the Confessor, *On the Cosmic Mystery of Jesus Christ*). This poem links perfectly the desire of the supernatural, the microcosm, and Proteus themes. The last two lines even synthesize the desire for the supernatural as both drive and lack: "If goodness lead him not, yet weariness/May toss him to my breast."

These are: first, gift without contrast; second, spirit and grace as inseparable; and third, the orientation of the *cosmos as such* to the supernatural — which renders it indeed "precisely reality," to echo Bresson.

But he also begins faintly to point to a fourth component, which more recent commentators have shown to be also present in the authentic tradition. This is the analogy between *grace* and *art*. One should recall that *charis* is a Greek word, implying a kind of divine embellishment (the "girdle of Venus") and arguably has no real Old Testament equivalent, any more than the *Torah* originally envisaged a supernatural elevation of humanity.

For Pico, as we have seen, the human spiritual creature, precisely *as* drawn beyond itself by grace, is self-constructing, just as, for Cusa and Bérulle, we "give ourselves to ourselves" just *because* we are through and through divine gift. Our 'autonomy' and openness is in fact the counterpart of a radical receptivity which renders even our own action at a higher level utterly passive. Thus we are, for Pico, cultural creatures beyond nature because we are also engraced creatures beyond nature. As de Lubac notes, this is much more specific in Cusa, who frequently discusses how humans inhabit their own 'conjectural' and projected world of signs, numbers, figures, and perspectives. In both thinkers though, something cultural is added to something cosmic, because no longer do humans merely reflect all elements of the cosmos as its microcosmic center; rather they occupy their own little world that stands out from the cosmos, because it conjectures also a relation to the supernatural beyond the cosmos. Usually this insistence is interpreted by Renaissance scholars as a new hubristic self-confidence in Man and his powers. De Lubac points out to the contrary that this shift of microcosmic reference from cosmic immanence to supernatural transcendence is an explicitly *Christian* shift, linked to acknowledgment of the supreme glory of God, and already present, for example, in Maximus the Confessor. Hence de Lubac begins to suggest a link between the paradoxically necessary (for human nature) vertical supplement of grace and the paradoxically necessary (for human nature) horizontal supplement of culture (event and sign).

The examples of the Renaissance thinkers are important to de Lubac in another way also, which again connects to his relation with Teilhard. They reveal how a fearless adoption of new scientific facts can enhance rather than destroy Christian allegory and our understanding of the supernatural. Cusa and later Bérulle took heliocentricism to mean that the earth was elevated by a noble star and Man its inhabitant elevated in consequence.[5] One aspect of this elevation, though, was a capacity to see and reflect upon the light of the sun and so to acknowledge also a radical dependency of the earth and humanity upon the solar center. Thereby the paradox of the supernatural now receives a more adequate cosmic counterpart: earth and man are elevated, but only as more radically receptive. In Bérulle, man retains fully his Piconian and Florentine nobility, yet his Protean character is linked to his created nothingness which is most exemplified by Christ, the true sun of creation, who is most eminently human just *because* his person, his intellectual *pneuma*, his *esse*, is wholly and utterly

5. *Pic de la Mirandole*, pp. 130-45.

divine. (In parallel to Pico it is Bérulle the mystic and *not* the later scholastics who most effectively elaborated Aquinas's Christological metaphysics of *"*one divine *esse"* — not two, divine and human — in Christ.)

The Supernatural in Relation to de Lubac's Other Theological Thematics

De Lubac's significant theological writings on other topics bear out the idea that he saw the paradox of grace as equally the paradox of culture and of human history. We can see this in three specific instances: evolution, scriptural exegesis, and ecclesiology.

In all three cases, as von Balthasar well points out, de Lubac follows the logic of a later and essential addition that nonetheless arrives from above as a gift and does not unfold ineluctably from below. So in the first instance, with Teilhard, he reads the early stages of evolution not so much as teleologically directed to the later ones but more as 'typologically' foreshadowing them. What to atheist eyes might then seem the merely chance and adventitious in later 'random' mutation is rather, to the theologian, the sign of a completion in some sense 'required' by what went before, but nonetheless supplied as a surprising gift.[1]

---

1. *Teilhard de Chardin: The Man and His Meaning*, trans. René Hague (New York: Hawthorn, 1965), *passim*.

The same logic governs the traditional 'fourfold exegesis', beginning with Origen.[2] Literal meanings foreshadow, but do not logically entail, higher 'mystical' meanings or later 'eschatological' ones. In insisting upon traditional allegory, de Lubac continued his battle against extrinsicism. Christ's human nature could not exhibit through divine personification the divine idiom unless the literal events of his life were doubled by an allegorical summation of all of the Old Testament and indeed all foregoing reality.[3] Only the meta-narrative level of allegory, which links events beyond causal connection, sustains the narrative coherence relevant to and constitutive of Christianity as such. (This is one reason why de Lubac exalts the allegorizing Erasmus above Luther and Calvin.) The allegorical narrative situates us within the world text (*not*, as for much Protestantism, hermeneutically outside it as 'interpreters'). We must continue to write that text through moral tropological performance, whose reaction to evil is only sustained in its goodness by a transmoral looking towards an anagogic plenitude of meaning beyond good and evil (because purely good) that is at once personal and mystical and yet collective and eschatological. (The assertion of the primacy of the mystical over the moral is exhibited elsewhere in de Lubac's creative response both to Nietzsche and to Buddhism.)[4]

2. *Medieval Exegesis,* vols. 1 and 2 (Grand Rapids/Edinburgh: Eerdmans/ T&T Clark, 1998 and 2000), *passim.* For a summation, see Henri de Lubac, *Scripture in the Tradition* [*L'Ecriture dans la Tradition*], trans. Luke O'Neill (New York: Herder and Herder, 1968).

3. *Medieval Exegesis 2,* pp. 83-125.

4. See, for this thematic, "Tripartite Anthropology," in *Theology in History* (San Francisco: Ignatius, 1996).

On the other hand, in accordance with the paradox of the supernatural, the movement of inspired reading is not entirely spiritual, or forwards and upwards. To suppose this would be to commit the *Joachite* error of spirit escaping from historical form: an error which de Lubac deemed to be especially heinous.[5] Every allegorizing exegesis also points backwards: if baptism 'fulfills' the crossing of the Red Sea it does not supersede the latter, but in part can *only* be expounded in terms of the latter. For allegory to work and be renewed we are always returned to the literal — just as, for the mystical path to be taken, we are always returned to the social, political, and ecclesial. *In* the literal resides the springs of spiritual plenitude, even though there is no exigency for the latter, just as the supernatural always eventuates as the fulfillment of the natural. The more exceeding the height, the greater the echo of the resounding deeps.

De Lubac confirms that his attitude here is that of the tradition by showing that, from Origen onwards, a 'scientific' interest in the history of the Bible — in date, time, place, authorship, etc. — could naturally go along with, and even reinforce, the interest in spiritual meaning. Accordingly, de Lubac hoped for a new future synthesis of biblical criticism with literary sensibility. (One can contrast

---

5. Henri de Lubac, *La Posterité Spirituelle de Joachim de Flore,* in 2 volumes (Paris: Aubier-Montaigne, 1979-1981). De Lubac's last work, written in his eighties, therefore concerned the danger of detaching *esprit* from both nature and the word. The simultaneous attack upon secular utopianism and over-spiritualizing pietism sustains his central paradox to the end. It also complements his genealogy of the pernicious effects of "pure nature" with a complementary genealogy of the equally deleterious consequences of "pure spirit."

this demand with the sterile interest of the 'Yale School' in the no-man's-land of "history-like narrative" which at once abolishes *real* history *and* ignores the essential allegorical underpinning of Christian doctrine.)

The same structure — down-to-up-and-down-again, back-to-forward-and-back-again — is seen in de Lubac's ecclesiology, which is almost as central to his *opus* as is the *surnaturel* thematic. Crucial to the linkage of the two is de Lubac's denial that an Augustinian integration of nature and grace encouraged any drift towards papalist theocracy and politicization of the spiritual in the later Middle Ages.[6] To the contrary, de Lubac shows that Giles of Rome's advocacy of papal coercive power was linked with an Averroism that construed even spiritual power in quasi-physical terms of a more intense literal force. By contrast, the Augustinian perspective saw the power of the Church as strictly spiritual and suasive, not as having any even indirect authority to intervene in civil coercive legality — for example to depose a head of state and promulgate a civil law. (But de Lubac arguably exaggerates this, and certainly — in understandable reaction to the Catholic right-wing *intégristes* — fails fully to grasp the notion of the Church as a replete society in Augustine's *Civitas Dei*.)[7] Even though the Church's authority was, strictly speaking, spiritual, its relevance stretched everywhere and it could have a view on even the smallest temporal particulars. This for de Lubac distin-

---

6. Henri de Lubac, "Autorité de L'Église en Matière Temporelle" [the article dates from the 1930s] in *Théologies d'occasion* (Paris: Désclee de Brouwer, 1984), pp. 217-40.

7. See the excellent article by P.-D. de La Soujeole, O.P., "Le débat sur le surnaturel et l'ecclésiologie contemporaine" in RT *Surnaturel*, pp. 329-44.

guishes Augustinian integration from later notions of an autonomous secular sphere where ecclesial interference might extend only to the laying down of general principles.

Here then also, while human social nature in its entirety can only be judged rightly in the light of the supernatural, the latter is not a sort of additional 'something' operating a theocratic usurpation of natural human debate and action.

Nor is the authority of grace within the Church something extrinsic and invisible, in contrast to visible church structures that can be justified on merely rational principles (often a post-Tridentine view). Instead it arrives intrinsically, in the symbolism and liturgy of the Eucharist which 'makes' the Church. Once again, authority here only arises from above (whether the episcopal hierarchy or the scriptures) and the future by returning us also to the below and to the past for legitimation.

The Eucharist, up to 1300 or so, remained, according to de Lubac, less a derivation from clerical power and a present miraculous spectacle than a re-presentation of the historical body of Christ.[8] The supernaturally spiritual was here not temporally prior, but rather first arose in the temporal mirror of individual spiritual digestion of eucharistic meaning. And again, this elevated moment was not for now to be persisted in, as its 'mysticism' only foreshadowed the collective mystical *eschaton*. After internal absorption comes once again the external, this time in the mode of the meritorious building up of the body of Christ which further realizes the eucharistic repetition of Christ's literal

8. *Corpus Mysticum: L'Eucharistie et L'Eglise au Moyen Age* (Paris: Aubier-Montaigne, 1949), *passim*.

historicity. Authority in the Church is therefore an hierarchical flow through time, not an alien imposition from a removed space in the present — whether this be the Counter-Reformation papacy or the typed, bound, and sealed Scriptures, bare of all commentary, promulgated by the Reformers.

6

De Lubac and
von Balthasar Contrasted

To gauge the importance of de Lubac's *surnaturel* thesis, it is important to situate it in relation to the rest of twentieth-century theology and philosophy.

First of all, the *nouvelle théologie* stood alongside and not apart from the revised neo-Thomism of Gilson and, to a degree, even that of Maritain. The latter's advocacy of "integral humanism" was close to de Lubac's heart and Maritain's notion of an intellectual intuition of *esse* was seen by de Lubac as near to his own metaphysics of *pneuma*. Finally, Maritain had refused the naturally sinless angels thesis, the rejection of which was also important for de Lubac.[1] The lay Catholic philosopher nonetheless retained serious reservations about the new picture of the *surnaturel*. Not so his fellow layman Etienne Gilson, who entirely endorsed it.[2] I have

---

1. De Lubac, *The Discovery of God*, trans. Alexandrer Dru (New York: P. J. Kennedy, 1960), p. 88; R. Mougel, "Le position de Jacques Maritain," in RT *Surnaturel*, pp. 73-98.

2. Etienne Gilson, *Letters to Henri de Lubac* (San Francisco: Ignatius, 1986), esp. p. 24.

already tried to show how Gilson's reaffirmation of the ontological difference (and demonstration, contra Heidegger, that this *can be* — and even can more coherently be — expressive of the creator/created difference) belongs naturally with de Lubac's reaffirmation of the natural desire for the supernatural.

Indeed, it can now be seen that the *Surnaturel* of 1946 was almost as important an event of cultural revision as *Being and Time* or the *Philosophical Investigations.* For it revealed that the space of modern philosophy and culture was paradoxically created by a dubious scholastic theology, which reinvigorated the primitive pagan ontological assumption that 'capacity' or 'power' rather than 'desire' will disclose reality to us.[3]

In the second place, there is the question of transcendental Thomism. Here it must be remembered that, for de Lubac's theological *longue durée,* the most *modern* philosophy is precisely neo-scholasticism, which tended to forget that "the soul is in a manner all things" and to reduce the role of the intellect to empiricist representation. By contrast, rationalist thinkers like Descartes, Kant, and Leibniz could be seen as half re-capturing the centrality of *pneuma,* whilst idealist thinkers like Hegel and Schelling could be seen as continuing the Christian Renaissance enterprise of philosophical theological integration, albeit in a half-debased gnostic and Behmenistic form. Hence de Lubac was certainly very influenced by the Belgian Jesuit Joseph Maréchal's 'Kantian'

---

3. See the fine elaboration of de Lubac's genealogy by J.-Y. Lacoste, "Le Desir et l'inexigible: Préambles à une Lecture" in *Les Études Philosophiques* 2 (1995): 223-46.

argument that Kant had not shown any genuine reasons to set bounds to cognitive speculation and the *a priori* reach of spirit — especially Maréchal's adoption of Jacobi's contention that speculation beyond finite bounds is necessarily constitutive of our apprehension even of the finite (this is akin to Cusa's 'conjecturing' model of human understanding).[4]

Nevertheless de Lubac saw Maréchal as too much divorcing spirit from its interaction with the material world. His master was rather Maurice Blondel, whose thesis concerned not the straining of spirit beyond finite bounds, but the inadequacy of theoretical understanding to grasp the willed concrete *acts* of the spirit, deemed by Blondel to be comprehensible only by reference to a supernatural lure. Following this model, de Lubac saw that spirit, in exceeding the cosmos and exceeding itself, is always already in practice drawn beyond itself by specific historical mediation. Its cultural self-excess is also the self-excess of grace reaching downwards. For this reason, de Lubac rejected Maréchal and Rahner's (still neo-scholastic) view that the natural orientation to the supernatural discloses merely the possibility of grace and not already something of its actuality. He rightly saw that in Rahner there is no paradoxical reaching of the finite towards the supernatural, only a transcendentalist reworking of Cajetan's "potential for obedience" on the one hand, and a reworking of Cajetan's grace-supplied natural desire for the supernatural (Rahner's "supernatural existential") on the other.[5]

---

4. *The Discovery of God*, pp. 65ff.

5. *The Mystery of the Supernatural*, trans. Rosemary Sheed (London: Herder & Herder, 1967), pp. 72ff., 138ff., 275ff.

De Lubac and von Balthasar Contrasted

In the third place, there is the question of the relation of the *nouvelle théologie* to neo-orthodoxy. De Lubac profoundly admired both Bonhoeffer and Barth. In many ways de Lubac's wartime emergency *Surnaturel* reaches parallel conclusions to Bonhoeffer's wartime emergency *Letters and Papers from Prison*. For both theologians grace must be sought in the ordinary; the majestic and the pious have now had their dubious day. On the other hand, Bonhoeffer's Lutheranism leads him to exalt a dialectical identity between the presence and absence of God. Thus he finally celebrates exactly what the *Surnaturel* refuses: an autonomous secularity grounded in a univocal ontology, *etsi Deus non daretur*.

De Lubac's admiration of Barth derived from his sense that Barth had gone some way towards re-inventing the kind of historical-literary exegesis of which he dreamed. Von Balthasar's critique of Barth, however, which develops the insights of de Lubac and of Przywara, marks the crucial meeting and parting of the ways in all Western twentieth-century theology.[6] No pure Barthianism has survived this encounter, even amongst insightful Protestants. For it became clear in the wake of this book that Barth's theology, for all its apparent innovation, remained confined within a Baroque contrast of nature with grace, and of reason with revelation, and had failed to reckon either with the *analogia entis* or the *surnaturel* as governing both philosophy and theology according to a logic rooted in a non-idolatrous understanding of the Creator-created divide.

6. Hans Urs von Balthasar, *The Theology of Karl Barth,* trans. John Drury (New York: Holt, Rinehart, and Winston, 1971), *passim*.

In this way, von Balthasar actually opened out the ecumenical significance of de Lubac's *surnaturel* thesis. But did he do full justice to it and provide in his own theology a fuller working out of de Lubac's deepest position? In many ways yes, but in some ways no.

A careful reading of von Balthasar's account of the supernatural in his Barth book suggests a certain divergence from de Lubac and a kind of Germanic Protestant residue in the Francophile Swiss theologian. Briefly, von Balthasar tends to shift the call of the supernatural towards a full identity with historically received grace, instead of seeing it as at once paradoxically 'pre-historical' and yet entirely orientated towards sacred history. In this fashion de Lubac's thesis starts to look more like a straightforward Barthian insistence on the primacy of revelation. Nevertheless, as we have seen, such a reading is consonant with those passages in *The Mystery of the Supernatural,* where, in seeking to square his views with *Humani Generis,* de Lubac reduces the natural desire for the supernatural to a negative lack and denies that it in any way positively anticipates the supernatural end.

The idea that von Balthasar reads de Lubac in a conservative and over-Barthian fashion is confirmed in several ways. First of all, von Balthasar celebrates the fact that, for Barth, nature is "totally locked up" and yet in this negativity "totally open to grace." This sounds more like Jansenius than the original de Lubac. Secondly, von Balthasar says that *theology* will tend to see the natural desire for the supernatural as a mere obediential potency, while *philosophy* will see it as an innate instinct. But this suggests that von Balthasar somehow thinks of theology as 'naturally Cajetanian' and of de Lubac's thesis as inherently somewhat transcendentalist and naturalistic! Thirdly, von Balthasar thinks that the transition from Maréchal to de Lubac is parallel to the transition from Schleiermacher to Barth. But surely the *surnaturel* thesis rather deconstructs the terms of the Schleiermacher/Barth divide? (And Maréchal is far nearer de Lubac than Schleiermacher is.)[7]

In these ways von Balthasar seems to edge de Lubac's position slightly towards a Barthian 'grace over-against nature'. This is conversely confirmed when he goes on to say that Rahner is *somewhat right* (as against de Lubac) to insist that the *natura pura* possesses a regulative value, not just, as for de Lubac, in order to point out that God created freely an animal like man, but also to guarantee, within the existing human essence, the gratuity of grace. (But von Balthasar is not consistent here; in his book on de Lubac, he actually upbraids the French master for conceding to *Humani Generis* a division between *pneuma* and the lure of supernatural!) For von Balthasar the issue is sometimes one of 'how much' to grant to grace and 'how much' to nature. But for de Lubac of course there can be no such question. Indeed that is the whole point.

It seems then that, despite his fundamental location within the "suspended middle," von Balthasar might have compromised this position in a way that is at once too Barthian *and* too Rahnerian.

A reading of his great trilogy can at times (only at times, yet at crucial times) confirm this.

First of all, there is the question of contrasting readings

---

7. Hans Urs von Balthasar, *The Theology of Karl Barth*, pp. 240-44.

of the Renaissance. For von Balthasar, Cusanus is the central historical enigma, and his brilliant but tortured exposition of Nicholas in *Herrlichkeit* accords in part with the reading of Cusa by de Lubac.[8] Yet von Balthasar, unlike de Lubac, sees in Cusa one root — perhaps the crucial one — of titanism. The always paradoxical French theologian, much more consistently than von Balthasar, insisted on a dialectical genealogy: it was *not*, according to de Lubac, the properly theological celebration of Man but the pious concern to conserve the gratuity of grace that engendered the monstrous titanic child of atheist humanism.

To sum up briefly this contrasting treatment of Cusanus: von Balthasar disliked the fact that, for Nicholas, Man as a second God echoes the divine *complicatio* and stands above the cosmic *explicatio* in his own created 'small world', whereas de Lubac (as we have seen) demonstrated rather just how specifically Christian this conception is. Somewhat in contradiction to this first point, von Balthasar also disliked Cusa's cosmic frame for a fusion of philosophy and theology, whereas de Lubac saw this as the Pauline apocalyptic subordination of all creation to deification and to the God-Man. As in the case of Eckhart, von Balthasar also worried about extreme 'identification' language in Cusa's mystical writings whereas de Lubac did not. (The passage to which von Balthasar objects in *De Filiatione Dei* actually clearly distinguishes our always "curved" mirrors from Christ's "straight" mirror in which we see God.) Von

8. Hans Urs von Balthasar, "The Knot: Nicholas of Cusa," in *The Glory of the Lord*, Vol. V: *The Realm of Metaphysics in the Modern Age*, trans. Oliver Davies et al. (Edinburgh: T&T Clark, 1991), 2.8.4.

Balthasar also worried that Christ as *maximum contractum* implies a dubious transfinite absolute; de Lubac did not express himself here, but against von Balthasar one can say that for Cusa there is an absolute transfinite humanity in Christ (like an absolutely infinite line that is still not a 'total' infinite — since it is not also an infinite square, circle, etc.) because of the communication of idioms consequent upon enhypostasization. The same contrast even extends to Bérulle: von Balthasar complains that the great Oratorian thinks he can ignore the tricky problems of metaphysics such as nominalism, where de Lubac suggests that his insistence on Christ's one divine *esse,* and consequent exploration of Christ's *états* as disclosive of fundamental ontological categories, opens up a new fusion of the historical and ontological.[9]

In the second place there is the question of the transition in von Balthasar from aesthetics to dramatics and an increasingly mythological rather than ontological register.

In his account of the aesthetic, von Balthasar rightly insists upon its objective formal properties of harmony and implicit hidden depth and its subjective properties of 'pleasing the sight' and ecstatically drawing us in to the reality which it discloses. Yet whereas de Lubac might have insisted on a to-and-fro between objective harmony (together with subjective pleasure stressing 'presence') on the one hand, and objective depth (together with subjective ecstasy suggesting *élan),* on the other, von Balthasar seems more absolutely to prioritize the forward direction from initial presence towards eventual ecstasy. Hence the first

9. *The Glory of the Lord,* Vol. V, 2.8.2.

pair — objective and subjective evidence — belongs to a "fundamental theology." Yet within *dogmatics proper,* a spiritual negative ecstasy corresponds to the way more historically specific persons and objects (and not just the general 'shape' of the objects of Christian devotion) lead us more and more towards acknowledgment of the divine personal 'other' who stands behind the attractively luring forms and freely shapes them.[10]

This then suggests that the passage from the aesthetics to the dramatics is a kind of dialectical advance in which the aesthetic is actually *left behind.* This reading of von Balthasar (at which many will protest) is confirmed in the *Theologic,* volume 1, where a Thomistic aesthetic holding of the balance between intellect and will is ultimately upset by a more Bonaventurian passage from the intellectual through the aesthetic to the 'higher' realm of will and love. It is also confirmed by the Preface to the *Theodrama,* where von Balthasar speaks of an action that lies beyond 'form' and the contemplatable — to which the *riposte* must be, how can there be an action at all, especially an action upon something, which does not in some sense appear and which is not regardable (whether or not it is 'comprehensible')?[11] Another way of putting this would be to point out that *praxis* must always include an element of transitive, expressive *poesis,* even if this be merely the manifestation and

10. *The Glory of the Lord,* Vol. I: *Seeing the Form,* trans. John Riches et al. (London: T&T Clark, 1988), *passim* and esp. I, VII, II and III.

11. Hans Urs von Balthasar, *Theologic I,* trans. Graham Harrison (San Francisco: Ignatius, 2002), I. A, B, C; II, A, B; III, C. 2; IV A, D; *Theodrama,* trans. Graham Harrison (San Francisco: Ignatius, 1988-90) [volumes numbers and page references given], 1: 15-23.

development of a thought in the mind, which is an 'inner word' for Augustine and Aquinas. The most discrete and fully accomplished act, which is that of intellectual comprehension, is still in principle an act which renders itself publicly available, as Wittgenstein insisted.

But under Balthasar's non-poetic view of action as something 'in excess' of form, the aesthetic aspect of drama must inevitably be instrumentalized. On a superficial reading one might suppose that von Balthasar's statement that drama fuses appearance, action, and discourse means that for him it gives equal weight to all three components. But a closer reading belies this. In the Preface to the *Theodrama,* von Balthasar declares that "it [drama] transforms the event into a picture that can be seen" — whereas to the contrary, the event specific to drama is already cinematic, the representative image is itself moving and itself acting (or plural images are moving and inter-acting). The event does not wait upon the spectacle of drama in order to become visible: it is already in principle visible, and what drama does is make an audience turn towards this visibility which is also on the stage 'frozen' and rendered repeatable. Von Balthasar is somewhat confusing as to when he is speaking of the conventional stage and when he is speaking rather of a *welttheater* in which we are participants rather than spectators, but the above quotation suggests that the 'spectacle' of stage drama gives visibility to the pure event of the real world-theatre. In that case the aesthetic in the mode of visible dramatic form is thoroughly instrumentalized.

This is confirmed by von Balthasar's view that the aesthetic, unlike the dramatic, is not interpersonal and interactive. Drama as interpersonal must mean either the real world-drama or else the internal dynamics of the stage; it cannot refer to the relation between a drama and its audience where the edge of the stage is conventionally inviolable. Clearly for Balthasar this 'passive spectacle' aspect of the theatre is coincident with its merely aesthetic aspect. But such a notion betrays a profoundly Kantian attitude to the aesthetic, where the paradigm of the beautiful is the lonely spectator looking at a picture, not the participant in a dance or the dweller within a building (to invoke Gadamer's critique of the Kantian paradigm).

If, in contrast to von Balthasar, one allows that one can actively 'play within' beauty as well as regard it, then the experience of the Beautiful can be seen as the mediation between the True and the Good. Often, in the first volume of *Theologic,* von Balthasar does take just this view. It is the inextricable involvement with beauty which ensures that the True is the making apparent of being *(alētheia)* and not a banal ontological tautology (as in "there is rain because there is rain"). It is equally the unavoidable detour via the Beautiful which ensures that the Good is the radiating of gift and not simply closed self-fulfillment. Yet in the end for von Balthasar, both here and in the Preface to the *Theodrama,* the logic and discourse of the True is rather what leads us *beyond* the appearance of the Beautiful to the ineffable personal call of the Good. And now it is the Good, not the Beautiful, which mediates: it renders God's glory beautiful because it ensures that it points beyond form to action received and responded to. Equally it renders divine utterance true because revealed beauty is ultimately reduced to an announcement of something which lies discreetly beyond itself. Thus we are told in the Preface, in a markedly Barthian fashion, that "the good which God brings about can only be explained and demonstrated from within itself, and will not allow itself to be dragged into the ambiguities of the *welttheater*. Not ultimately." Penultimately, for von Balthasar, God is so dragged in, but then his appearance in our ambivalent drama seems to fall under a dialectical contradiction, as God becomes sin and death for the sake of our redemption. This tendency to reduce God's performance in our drama to the Lutheran adoption of a role *sub contrario* — as opposed to positive and ontologically continuous aspects of kenosis and transfiguration — seems to entail also the instrumentalization of beauty and a forgetting of the *analogia entis*. For what becomes ultimate within this perspective is the invisible divine decree and our interior response to it. (The lack of any real historical, political, and ecclesial dimension to Balthasar's dramatics fits with this picture.)

De Lubac less often entertained this sort of voluntarism (although it was indicated that one can detect a voluntarist/intellectualist hesitation in *The Mystery of the Supernatural*).

Von Balthasar's division between a 'fundamental' and a 'dogmatic' theological aesthetics (reflecting his voluntarist streak) is echoed more broadly by his divisions between a 'general' philosophical, metaphysical aesthetics on the one hand and a 'special' theological aesthetics on the other. One can argue that such a division is alien to the spirit of de Lubac, and that von Balthasar entertains it just because he ultimately encourages an abandonment of the metaphysics of cosmic harmony in favor of a gnostic hypostasization of the violence of the Cross. De Lubac, unlike von Balthasar, sees Pico and Cusa's cosmic perspective as a more fully theistic (rather than one-sidedly personalist) one, yet not at all as neglectful of the moments of rupture and redemption, which also possess their cosmic dimensions.

The consequence of von Balthasar's Bonaventurian/ Barthian outlook is fully apparent in his Trinitarian theology and Christology. Here dogmatics floats free of all speculative ontology analogically rooted in our natural powers of comprehension, as de Lubac's perspective would require. The ontological difference is forgotten when von Balthasar speaks of a real "gain" to the Trinity from the suffering humanity of Jesus (even if for von Balthasar the Trinity has decided to receive from the Creation what it might have received within itself). The simplicity of God is forgotten when von Balthasar (against the Lateran declaration of 1215) speaks of the Father as handing over "the entire substance" of the Godhead to the Son, such that the divine essence remains in a kind of suspense. The personal character of the divine essence as such (which the Russians tried to accentuate through the concept of Sophia) is forgotten when von Balthasar so reduces the Trinitarian persons to free centers of being (forgetting that the Son is entirely the Father's objective *verbum;* the Spirit entirely the Paternal-filial objective *donum*) that *by dialectical inversion* they become subject to an impersonal negative logic of the essence emptied of all personality. Hence in order for the Son to be free there arises (this is pure Schelling) a kind of shadow of rupture between the Father and the Son which the Spirit both preserves and heals.[12]

---

12. Hans Urs von Balthasar, *Theodrama,* 4: 235-37; 336-85; 3: 183-92; 489-521.

De Lubac and von Balthasar Contrasted

The supersession of polytheism and the unity of the Trinitarian action *ad extra* is forgotten when von Balthasar speaks of the Spirit in the economic realm (treated as if ontically 'other' to the immanent Trinity) as deciding skittishly to jump into a middle position in order to transmit the *hypostasis* of the *Logos* to Jesus' humanity and later to 'remind' the Father and the Son of the shadow of possible rupture that has always hovered over them. For von Balthasar, this mythicized Spirit then intimates that now the rupture and paternal rejection must be cashed out if Father and Son wish dialectically to sustain their eternal love and yet redeem mankind. There is no consideration here of the fact that the radicalism of the doctrine of substantive relation already allows that, in the eternal *taxis,* the 'acting back' of the Spirit upon the Son is supplementarily original with the very generation of the Son, who is indeed breathed out as Word in the breath of the *Pneuma*. Hence the Spirit's 'taking the lead' in the order of the economy, insofar as the action of the entire Trinity upon the humanity of Jesus is 'appropriated' to the Spirit, does not cancel its procession *per Filium*. The transformative action of the Spirit can only be upon Christ's humanity and not upon his personhood (a fact von Balthasar ignores), since the latter is impassable. Nevertheless, the personhood of Christ can also actively receive this action just insofar as it is eternally constituted, through an essential reflux, by the Spirit which proceeds through it.

The narrative as well as ontological subtlety of Aquinas (or Bérulle) is forgotten, when von Balthasar substitutes a rupture between Father and Son for a tension between Christ's divine and his human nature. The angelic doctor is accused of supposing that the higher part of Christ's human soul is immune to the distress of the Passion while enjoying the beatific vision. Yet Aquinas to the contrary insisted that the *whole humanity of Christ* both underwent the Passion and continued to enjoy the vision. The lower sensory part of the soul suffered according to its proper object, but by conjunction with the higher intellectual part, it was suffused with the beatific vision, while the inverse applied to the upper aspect: it directly and perfectly rejoiced while indirectly suffering. Moreover, Aquinas suggested that the downward influence was (since Christ remained on earth) more dominant than the upwards one.[13]

But by supposing that not just Christ's intellectual soul but also his eternal personhood was implicated in suffering, von Balthasar confuses the personal with the conscious, and the hypostatic (which is, as it were, hyper-pneumatic — though Christ possessed a human *pneuma*) with the psychic.

This projected mythic-gnostic spectacle theatrically 'over-against us' seems to deliver the latent danger of von Balthasar's Barthian tendency. Inversely, the 'Rahnerian' tendency is shown in the foundational prologue to the theological aesthetics where an appeal to a set of initial appearances seems to be just a necessary entry point given the subjective circumstances of our human understanding, which is later to be left behind. This is then somewhat equivalent to the 'supernatural existential' and introduces a dubious contrast between a kind of theological *a priori* on the one hand and an empirical theological content on the other. The latter is then likely to become too positive and

13. ST III. Q. 10, a2; Q. 45, a7.

ontic in character. One should rather say that, since revelation is the arrival in time of *esse* as such (not an *ens*) which elevates our entire ontic nature, that its impact is therefore indissolubly subjective and objective, general and particular. It follows that foundation is dogmatics and dogmatics is foundation.

A second 'Rahnerian' element is arguably evident in von Balthasar's elaboration of a metaphysical ontology prior to theology. De Lubac never engaged in such an endeavor: for him the simplest proofs of God's existence are true, but true for spirit in some way conscious of its participation in divine illumination. As we have seen, this for de Lubac already involves an onlook to the supernatural and so an anticipation of actual grace. (Despite this 'Rahnerian' element, von Balthasar is also elsewhere unfair to Rahner, since he judges his discourse on *Geist* by Barthian, not Lubacian standards.)

Von Balthasar's notion that the Creation can truly give something to God also suggests a more independent ontological space for Creation than de Lubac would allow. As we have seen, de Lubac's theory of the supernatural seeks to remain with the paradox that God who is all in all yet brings about a not-God to share in his nature. Here de Lubac is close to the mystery that God is the God who can be outside himself — and therefore is the God who elevates creatures into deity — a notion explored more rigorously by the Russian Sophianic tradition, especially Bulgakov, than by von Balthasar. Indeed in his commentary on Teilhard's poem "The Eternal Feminine," de Lubac (though he cautiously distances himself from Bulgakov) more or less sees the *surnaturel* as a kind of cosmically dif fused feminine presence and receptive passivity. One can add that the Sophianic theology is clearly the product of a tradition that had scarcely known (except as an alien import) the Western rupture between nature and grace.

7

Thomistic Criticisms of de Lubac on the Supernatural: The Aesthetic Compromise

We shall see in this chapter how von Balthasar's reinvocation of the aesthetic is central for current Thomistic debate about the supernatural.

First of all though, one should be aware that there remain several long-standing objections to de Lubac's thesis which are still invoked, both by die-hard neo-Thomists and by the much more sophisticated new Freibourg-Toulouse school of Dominican Thomists which has (in various degrees) modified its traditional neo-Thomism to accommodate certain *nouvelle théologie* perspectives. (One problem with all these debates is that they seem worryingly to revert to the view that what Aquinas thinks is necessarily decisive.)

To rehearse briefly these criticisms. First of all, truly die-hard neo-Thomists like Lawrence Feinberg still insist that de Lubac's thesis is an essentially Scotist one. As we shall see in the next chapter, de Lubac himself did not make an adequate distinction between Aquinas and Scotus on this matter. However, recent scholarship rather identifies Scotus as one source of the long-term drift towards *natura pura*. For Scotus, the term "supernatural" reverts (almost as with the pagan Greeks) to a qualification only of God and of divine action: our desire for the supernatural and even possession of grace is wholly natural. He denies that this natural desire is 'elicited' by intellectual curiosity, merely because, for Scotus, the will has primacy and is always more truly its own ultimate principle.[1] The will is for him naturally orientated to the supernatural because by nature the human intellect can grasp univocal being as such in independence of its spiritual or material instantiation. Thus by nature we are adapted to see spiritual being and even God, who, although infinite, still falls within the quasi-generic divisions of simple existence. After the Fall, this natural capacity must be restored by grace — along with our apprehension of the genuine univocal ontology. But we only truly receive an anticipation of the beatific vision in its supernatural specificity in the first place through the work of grace. Hence already grace has become here somewhat extrinsic and explicitly does not involve deification, which is an intrinsic raising of our finite nature.[2]

De Lubac's thesis is therefore more Thomist than Scotist (and we shall see further reasons to assert this in the next chapter).

Secondly, there is the thorny problem of the souls in limbo who enjoy a purely natural beatitude. This appears to be accentuated by Aquinas, as Serge-Thomas Bonino of

1. Duns Scotus, *Ordinatio* I. Prol. pars I, Quinta; IV, d. 49; Q. 10, no. 2.

2. Duns Scotus, *Quodlibet* 17, a2 [4.] 7, and see Olivier Boulnois, "Surnaturel," in *Dictionnaire Critique de Théologie*, ed. J.-Y. Lacoste (Paris: PUF, 1998).

Toulouse argues, since the Thomist souls of babies in limbo are the happiest lost boys and girls in the whole of mediaeval theology. They simply do not know what they have missed, whereas even Dante's souls of unbaptized babies sigh with Bonaventurian melancholy when Dante and Vergil pass by. However, one cannot rule out the interpretation which would say that these souls are happily unaware of a natural desire for the supernatural which remains eternally frustrated. Limbo is still a state of human imperfection. And in a sense Aquinas's admirably compassionate humanism might be said to leave the souls of unbaptized babies eternally as *baby-souls* playing idly and creatively throughout all ages.[3]

In the third place, there is the issue of a human natural love for God, independent of supernatural grace, of which Aquinas indeed speaks. However, it is notable that, for Aquinas, we share this love even with non-sentient beings. They exercise it insofar as they are part of a whole or the common good of the whole universe which is God himself.[4] De Lubac had grounds for thinking that this was not a fully free and personal love, but rather that spontaneous animal affection which for Aquinas (here very Aristotelian) is nonetheless exercised by us at a more conscious intellectual and voluntary level. It is clear from elsewhere in Aquinas that this is *not* the whole of the return to God that an intellectual

---

3. Serge-Thomas Bonino O.P., "La théorie des limbes et le mystère du surnaturel chez saint Thomas d'Aquin," in RT *Surnaturel*, pp. 131-66; Aquinas, *De Malo*, Q. 5 a3 ad I. My interpretation here was already put forward in another old article which built up towards de Lubac's *Surnaturel*: E. Brisbois, "Désir naturel et vision de Dieu," in *Nouvelle Révue Théologique* 54 (1927): 96-97.

4. ST I. II. Q. 109, a3.

creature *naturally* makes; rather the fully natural return of a spirit paradoxically involves a gratuitous divine raising of it above its own nature.

In the fourth place there is the fact, ably discussed by Jean-Pierre Torrell of Freibourg, that Aquinas, while he does not speak of *natura pura, does* speak of *pura naturalia.* Torrell does not make the mistake of confounding the two: he acknowledges with de Lubac that there is no identifiably discrete and *unified* pure nature in Aquinas, as there is in Cajetan. The plural mood is not incidental. Nevertheless, Aquinas does say that God could have created human beings in *pura naturalia* — these seem to include especially higher animal functions such as building houses and planting vines.[5] De Lubac's question here would be, would these purely natural humans have been the same animals? A resounding 'no' seems justified by Aquinas's statements (not discussed by Torrell) that if human beings possessed only a natural end they would be *less* than all other creatures, because then they would fail to make in their own natural mode (here intellectual) a full return to the Godhead.[6] Presumably this situation — and I think that here Torrell would concur — would be a highly *inappropriate* one, at the very least.

Moreover, Torrell mentions that from the list of 'natural' activities cited by Pseudo-Augustine in *Hypgnostikon* (III. IV.5) Aquinas seems to *omit* the higher functions like making friends and writing. Yet Torrell lends more inter-

5. *Quodlibet* I. Q4, a3 [8]. See also ST I. II. Q. 109, a2; Q. 114, a2; Jean-Pierre Torrell, O.P., "Nature et Grace chez Thomas d'Aquin," in RT *Surnaturel,* pp. 167-202.

6. SCG III. 25 [5].

pretative weight to the original list — as if Aquinas were implicitly invoking its entire contents — than to Aquinas's omissions from it. However, one could argue to the contrary that the latter is the most telling (and in any case the supposed allusion to the Pseudo-Augustinian text is but a likely supposition).

Torrell argues, with some textual demonstration, that *natura integra* before the Fall refers in Aquinas to the non-impairment of the *pura naturalia* and not to the entire intact natural/supernatural ordering. However, this disputed question may not be decisive. For Aquinas still insists — as Torrell mentions — that before the Fall no original justice was possible without grace.[7] This statement, since it *does* concern the entire natural/supernatural ordering, must then assume hermeneutic priority. Such priority then seems clearly to imply that, while one can point to many practices and virtues that do not of themselves require grace, they nevertheless cannot be exercised rightly (or at least with complete rightness), outside a more fundamental orientation of the entire realm of natural practices to the human supernatural destiny. (It is arguable that this then indicates — whether or not Aquinas recognizes the fact — that his nature/grace distinction can only be a very loose, relative affair.)

Torrell, like others (for example his pupil Gilbert Narcisse) within the Freibourg-Toulouse School, appears not really to allow an innate natural desire for the supernatural but only a variant of the Cajetanian *potentia obedi-*

7. ST I. Q. 100, a1 ad 2; *De Veritate* Q. 16, a1 ad 12; *De Malo* Q. 4, a2 ad I; Q. 5, a1 ad 13.

entialis. (In Aquinas this notion itself indicates an active dynamism.)[8]

Nonetheless, both Torrell and Narcisse want to say a little more, and this can be dubbed 'the aesthetic compromise'.

Reginald Garrigou-Lagrange and other neo-Thomists had already made much of Aquinas's use of arguments based on *convenientia* or 'appropriateness' rather than ontological or else demonstrable necessity. For Garrigou-Lagrange these arguments were something like 'probable' demonstrations. Torrell and Narcisse however (with many others) have rightly pointed out that *convenientia* in Aquinas is an *aesthetic* term — more to do with ontological 'fittingness' than with epistemological likelihood. It is at this point that their subtly revised neo-Thomism can half join forces with von Balthasar's aesthetic theology — as Narcisse indeed attempts — insisting (as I would agree) that von Balthasar's account of the *surnaturel* is less drastically radical than that of de Lubac.[9]

For neo-Thomists, whether palaeolithic or modified, there can be no rational demonstration of the arrival of grace on the basis of the natural desire for the supernatural. They contrast Aquinas's view that, while immortality

8. Torrell, and Narcisse, "Le Surnaturel dans la théologie contemporaine" in RT *Surnatural.* See also, Gilbert Narcisse O.P., *Les Raisons de Dieu: Argument de Convenance et Esthétique théologique selon Saint Thomas d'Aquin et Hans-Urs von Balthasar* (Fribourg: Editions Universitaries Fribourg Suisse, 1997). In addition, see Olivier-Thomas Venard, *Litérature et Théologie: Une saison en enfer* (Geneva: Ad Solem, 2002). Venard (of Toulouse), the most gifted and speculative of this school, construes 'the aesthetic compromise' in a way entirely compatible with de Lubac, and so not as a compromise at all.

9. Narcisse, "Le Surnaturel dans la théologie contemporaine."

can be demonstrated from the nature of the soul, the desire of the body for immortality is only a probable ground for the likelihood of resurrection.[10] The natural desire for the supernatural is seen as similarly only pointing in a remotely probable way to the actuality of the gift of grace. But as we have seen, de Lubac himself claimed that the (paradoxically) 'absolute' requirement of a divine gift could only be fully known by faith and not by reason — adding that there may scarcely be any reason not already inflected by faith.

However, for the Freibourg-Toulouse School the 'probability' is also an ontological fittingness. In that case, there is *some* sort of actual anticipation of the supernatural end in the structures of human nature that exceeds a mere formally latent possibility. Can there be a clear distinction between the 'aesthetic compromise' and de Lubac's thesis?

No and Yes. If the 'convenience' of human nature for supernatural elevation (which Aquinas certainly envisages) realizes a disposition of the divine *potentia ordinata* that nevertheless participates in and so reveals the eternal actuality and *potentia activa* of the divine *ars*, then the answer is no. For in that case convenience betokens a certain 'aesthetic necessity'. While it does not display a Leibnizian calculus of "the best structure" according to the infinite rules of *mathesis* (known only to God), it still displays more than an incidentally adopted set of means. The latter interpretation would reduce the aesthetic to the pragmatic and would tie beauty only to the willed pursuit of practical

---

10. See Lawrence Feinberg, *The Natural Desire to See God according to St. Thomas and His Interpreters* (Rome: Apollinare Studi, 2001), p. 549.

ends. Yet for Aquinas beauty mediates the cognitive and the desiring orders; as linked to the latter, the divine decision that convenience reflects is a matter of subjective judgment, not of objective calculation. As linked to the former this decision is still a matter of 'the best', or rather of *one optimum* given that infinity (as Aquinas insists) is compatible with multiple *optima*.

And where the *convenientia* of human nature for supernatural elevation intrinsically participates in the divine wisdom, then (since theory and practice are, in a theological perspective, inseparable for Aquinas) human nature must also be teleologically drawn towards the *eschaton* of beatitude that, nonetheless, it cannot elicit.

This, I would contend, is the only possible valid way to take Aquinas's aesthetics. Yet if, on the other hand, *convenientia* is read more extrinsically as simply the way an already replete human nature can appropriately lend itself to a further end and purpose added on to it by God — as if, for example, a railway carriage turned out to be an ideal home for gypsies after the closure of the branch line, and a ruling government proclaimed that this had always been secretly envisaged by the earlier government that built railways in the first place — then 'the aesthetic compromise' parts company with the *nouvelle théologie*.

But in that case also, the compromise is not really aesthetic. As with von Balthasar at times (times which this perspective unsurprisingly tries to invoke) a 'beauty' which is the mere sign of a contingently willed order self-deconstructs its initial seduction into a later realization that what one was really taken with was a well-oiled machine, excellently adapted to its purpose, but not intrinsically participating in or showing forth that purpose in advance. In that case the final willed end does not seem to be intrinsically beautiful, nor does our rational grasp of that end (and of our ordering to the beatific vision, of the offer of salvation) seem to require a perpetual — rather than initial — exercise of aesthetic judgment.

For de Lubac (and von Balthasar much of the time) the approach of God lay in beauty because God was eminently beautiful. To say this was only one way of spelling out the *surnaturel* thesis. But on this issue, proponents of the Freibourg-Toulouse School remain at times ambivalent, insofar as they remain also ambivalent as to their embrace of the primacy and ultimacy of the beautiful.

8

Aquinas and the Radicalization of de Lubac's Account of the Supernatural

By contrast with the Freibourg-Toulouse School, other recent (mainly lay) Catholic historians of philosophy and theology, often linked to an interest in phenomenology (Courtine, Boulnois, Marion, Schmutz, Lacoste), have tended to confirm a more radical reading of de Lubac and to argue that such a reading can be rooted in Aquinas himself. They stress the three components that I have already identified: first, spirit as intrinsically linked to grace; second, the entire *cosmos* as drawn through humanity to beatitude; third, grace as gratuitous because a gift can be a gift without contrast to gift.

In addition, in some cases they further develop a fourth theme of the grace/art analogy and a fifth theme concerning grace as causality on the model of 'unilateral exchange' (see below).

It is crucial here to recall (as we have to some degree regarding Scotus) recent research indicating that while de Lubac overlooked several mediaeval anticipations of the *natura pura*, Aquinas was actually the most radically free of these and cleaved most intensely (amongst thirteenth-century Catholic theologians) to the patristic vision.

So whereas in 1950 de Lubac was regarded as an Augustinian and only dubiously Thomistic, today, for very stringent reasons, one can say that he was both Augustinian and Thomist. The reasons are basically twofold. First of all, it is highly significant that Aquinas, almost uniquely amongst his contemporaries, insisted that Adam was created from the outset *with* the reception of grace. He did not live for a second under a regime of pure nature. For Bonaventure, by contrast, there was a short temporal interval, even though the Franciscan theologian certainly never envisaged a serious possibility of humanity without grace. This 'interval' was also retained by Peter Olivi and Duns Scotus.[1]

The second reason is more technical. Jacob Schmutz has suggested — with exhaustive documentation — that we should now see the transition in the understanding of the supernatural as but one aspect of a vaster change in the comprehension of all causality and particularly divine causality. This thesis concentrates round a shift in the meaning of the word *influentia*. Until 1250 or so *influentia* was linked with neoplatonic notions of *processio* and remained true to its metaphorical base. Divine influence (but also finite influence) was literally an *in-fluentia*, a "flowing in" of something higher to something lower to the degree that it could

---

1. See Torrell, "Nature et Grace chez Thomas d'Aquin," in RT *Surnaturel,* pp. 167-202; Boulnois, "Surnaturel," in *Dictionnaire Critique de Thœlogie,* ed. J.-Y. Lacoste (Paris: PUF, 1998); and Jacob Schmutz, "La Doctrine médiévale des causes et la théologie de la nature pure (XIIIe-XVIIe siècles)," in RT *Surnaturel,* pp. 217-64.

be received. On this model, the 'general' divine activity is indissociable from God's 'special' activity, his overall from his particular providence. Furthermore, another dimension of 'radical gift' or of gift without contrast, is herein disclosed. The creative influence of God does not influence creation, but posits creation as influence (it is 'a gift of a gift to a gift'). In this sense, it is radically unilateral. Yet it is paradoxically *so* unilateral that it gives even the recipient and the possibility of her gratitude. Indeed a radical gift must be of gratitude, since outside gratitude (the worshiping 'return' of all things to their source, from which they alone have existence) there is no finite *esse*. (Aquinas is clear that all creatures as existing acknowledge and praise God in some fashion.) Hence just to the degree that radical gift is unilateral, it is also involved in an exchange. And one can note here that the objection to de Lubac which insists that if, in any sense, grace is 'due' to us, in justice it cannot be a gift, is parallel to the objection to Marcel Mauss that any gift expecting a return gift cannot be a true gift. The implication of the *influentia* model is that, at the ontological level, this contrast of free unilateral gift with gift-exchange is surpassed (even though it would have to be seen as a "coincidence of opposites").[2]

It is surpassed because of radical hierarchy. Since the original 'thing' (Being, intelligence, soul, beauty, goodness, truth, unity, etc.) is fully received from the highest level by the lower levels according to their capacity for reception, it is the very alien gift itself that becomes what is proper to

---

2. Schmutz, "La Doctrine mediévale." See also SCG III. 20 and SCG III. 20-21, where the divine likeness is said to be in us *by causality*.

these lower levels. Hence God is the single influence, the single unilateral and total cause of everything. Yet since he causes by sharing his own nature, by giving his gifts to-be, the lower levels exert within their own sphere their own secondary and equally total causality. This is a kind of "exchange without reciprocity." There is reciprocity in the Trinity, and reciprocity within the Creation, but not between the Creation and God, because even though there is 'exchange' in the sense that creatures receive by returning, God properly receives nothing.

One can speak then of a paradoxical 'unilateral exchange'. Within this model, the unilateral influence is not general in the sense of establishing an overall determining parameter (like a set of laws or prevailing conditions) within which 'the exchange' or finite causality would operate, with a restricted scope for variation. To the contrary, the determining is here only established (creative cause within the Creation) in and with the determined, the general only as the sum of specific instances, even though it is a *dynamis* in excess of those instances.

For this older view then, there is never any competition between divine and finite causality according to a 'zero-sum' game of struggle for a single shared territory. This applied also, as Schmutz shows, to the possession of habitual grace; equally to the sphere of the drawing of human nature towards the supernatural end; and finally to the beginnings of the workings of actual grace in human nature. In these three respective instances for Aquinas: first, God causes deification and our free response, yet grace is entirely created (else it would occupy an impossible ontological limbo) and our deified transformation is in one sense entirely the work of our will; second, our innate tendency to beatitude is still God's supplementary gift in us; third, divine election is manifest intrinsically as the *praemotio physica* towards grace invading even our animality.[3]

However, Schmutz also shows that, as early as the thirteenth century, this model was disturbed. *Influentia,* by a "disassociation of sensibility" (to echo T. S. Eliot), started to mean simply an extrinsic conditioning, as when one says "I was much influenced by that person." However profound the effect, one may not be thinking here of a kind of spermatic "flowing-in." On the older, fundamentally Proclean model, the higher and especially the highest cause is always more deeply active at a lower level than any secondary cause. Aquinas says this about divine *esse: esse est intimus quam ea quae ipsum determinant.*[4] But on the newer view, a higher cause operating on a lower level is just 'one other' causal factor — like homework set by a teacher for the evening which is only one factor, alongside the demands of boyfriends and girlfriends, what's on downtown, etc., determining how the evening will actually be spent. It is quite *unlike* the instructions of a mystical master which might 'inform' the entire way one spent the evening.

By a gradual shift (part of the general rejection of Procleanism, except in Germany and before its Renaissance revival) the newer model started to prevail in the later Middle Ages. Divine causality began to be thought of as a 'general' influence, sometimes supplemented by 'special' influ-

---

3. ST I. II. Q. 112, aa2-3.
4. ST I. Q. 105, a5. Contrast Scotus, *Opus Oxoniense,* dist. 1, Q. 1: *esse simpliciter est proprius effectus Dei . . . videtur esse falsa.*

ences — miracles and the action of grace. Both these divine influences then collaborated with finite specific causes in a shared *concursus,* which involved a real dividing and ruling on the same ontic plane. Duns Scotus, because he rejected the view that *esse* as such was an effect of divine creation (rather than a thing's existence in this way or that), already thought that infinite and finite causes could collaborate within a single univocal field of operation. Hence he derided the older view that the higher cause gave being and form to the second cause as equivalent to supposing that the heart wrote letters on paper without the additional work of the hand.[5] From this example one can see, not only how questionable it might be to apply the case of an inner-ontic interaction to the ontological/ontic one, but also how (according to the older view) the latter 'informs' even the former. For one could argue that in a sense the 'heart' or the mind *does* do all the work of writing a letter, and hand and heart do not 'collaborate' in the way pen and paper do. (Surely Wittgenstein would have agreed with Aquinas and not Scotus here?)

Because he had adopted a new *concursus* model, Scotus claimed that, while the first cause produces an effect more universally than the second, it is not *prius* to it, but *simul* with it. Much later, thinkers went so far as to say that in some specific instances the divine causality was only 'secondary'.[6]

5. Scotus, *Ordinatio* I, dist. 36, q. *Unica,* no. 65. This passage is cited and discussed by Schmutz, in "La Doctrine mediévale." Contrast Aquinas at SCG III. 147 [6] discussing causality in grace: "Indeed, the cutting of the lumber results from the saw according to the essential character of its own form, but the form of the bench comes from the skilled mind which uses the tool."

6. See Schmutz, "La Doctrine mediévale."

Jacob Schmutz contends that the new conception eventually gives rise to all the interminable squabbles concerning the supernatural and grace, since now indeed one asks, "what share is human?" and "what share is divine?" A 'natural' opening to the supernatural or to grace *must* now amount to an elicitation of grace — hence it was either disallowed or else allowed with Pelagian implications. Because he already saw divine grace as merely special and extrinsic, William of Ockham entirely denied any innate human desire for the supernatural, and already (before Cajetan) linked this denial with a purged Aristotelianism: a natural desire for an end would be equivalent to a natural access to an end, even in theology. Ockham's extrinicism, linked to the priority of the divine *potentia absoluta,* even went so far as to say that God might have saved us without grace — by sheer decree or else as a reward for deemed merit. This opened him up to accusations of Pelagianism, by a dialectic which well reveals how a doctrine of pure nature compromises and does not protect the genuine gratuity of grace.

The de-metaphorization of 'influence' entailed then also a dissolution of the paradox of 'unilateral exchange'. Divine and finite causes now held to their own spheres and degrees of potential: hence they were unilateral acts entering into a kind of covenant for mutual purposes. One had now a mode of ontological contract rather than ontological gift-exchange. On the other hand, there was now also a dubious reciprocity (and potentially a sacrificial calculus) pertaining between an ontically reduced God on the one hand and ontic creatures on the other.

The loss of this paradox reveals a further dimension to the emergence of *natura pura.* De Lubac already saw that modern 'philosophy' was defined by this emergence, whereas antique philosophy tended to defer — by ascetic practice, myth, ritual, and *agnosis* — to an unknown divine wisdom. However, if 'pure nature' only emerged within the *concursus* model, where it was involved in a 'zero-sum competition' with the supernatural, then we can further see that only a theological shift defines the *hidden axioms* of what we now take to be philosophy as such. As François Laruelle has pointed out (failing to see that this applies mainly to *modern* philosophy, not to neoplatonism, nor to Catholic speculative theology/philosophy), we take philosophy to mean the supposed discovery of fixed general *conditioning* circumstances within which the conditioned must operate.[7] Laruelle suggests that all such 'discoveries' (including postmodern versions like those of Heidegger, Derrida, or Deleuze where the general conditions are anarchic) only ever have the status of plausible fictions. He further points out that, according to these hidden axioms, what is supposed to be 'fundamental' and determining (since, one can add, it is not a higher donating eminent cause, as for Aquinas) can only be epistemologically conceived (and so, given an immanentist assumption, also ontologically conceived with any true warrant) as 'belonging to' what it determines. Determining and determined are, in consequence, locked into a closed *speculative* structure which undermines the more than fictional status of its

---

7. François Laruelle, *Principes de la Non-philosophie* (Paris: PUF, 1996); "Qu'est ce que la non-philosophie?" in Juan Diego Blanco, *Initation à le Pensée de François Laruelle* (Paris: L'Harmattan, 1997), pp. 13-69. For de Lubac on pure nature and philosophy, see *Pic de la Mirandole* (Paris: Aubier-Montaigne, 1974), pp. 117-18.

components. Laruelle sees this structure as also a kind of contractual reciprocity projected onto the ontological plane. He tries to think instead a 'non-philosophy' under different axioms, in which the determining would only be posited along with the determined and there would be a kind of 'unilateral exchange' (as he terms it), an ontological projection of radical gift, gift without contrast.

But the *Surnaturel* of 1946, when one follows through its trajectory, along with Gilson's recovery of a theological ontological difference, already discloses that Christian theology *is* just such a 'non-philosophy'. The divine gift descending exceeds conditioning/conditioned specularity, just as the aspiring *élan* to the supernatural exceeds the contractual reciprocity of immanent being and opens to view a 'non-ontology', or what Claude Bruaire calls an 'ontodology'.

However, Schmutz also gives further reasons for arguing that this 'non-philosophy' or 'ontodology' is specifically Thomist as well as Augustinian. Franciscan theologians are often described as 'Augustinian'; yet Peter Olivi and Duns Scotus were amongst the most important instigators of the new 'specular' *concursus* view of causality which belongs together with the drift towards a univocalist ontology. And even Bonaventure was an early instigator, as Schmutz shows. For the Franciscan general, divine illumination of the human mind was no longer by causal influence, but rather by a general influence that permits the uncreated light to *concur* with the human soul. Moreover, this influence now no longer so clearly disclosed something of the divine intellect. In the act of knowledge we know the willed divine influence but not *ipsam rationem aeternam*: not something of those reasons themselves. Likewise in the field of practical reason, Bonaventure says that man can do good by his own force with only the help of the divine general *concursus*. Here already there is opened to view the model that will later be represented by metaphors of two men pulling one barge and so forth, and Schmutz notes that Adolf Harnack astutely saw in Bonaventure a beginning of semi-Pelagianism.[8] The logic that Bonaventure applied to illumination in general, he applied also to the *lumen fidei*, where he spoke of a divine 'special' influence, in contrast to his 'general' one. But here he was essentially following the lead of his teacher, Alexander of Hales, who had spoken of the natural *concursus* as being at work even in the case of *gratia superinfusa*. In the case of both general and specific divine causality, a sphere of independent and partial causality has been reserved for the creature. And this is already the space of *natura pura*.

It is thus evident that Aquinas was *more* Augustinian than the 'Augustinians' in refusing, or at least heavily restricting, the place of anything like 'pure nature'. It is also evident that this restriction was linked to a greater adherence to a neoplatonic sense of understanding as participation and an Augustinian understanding of illumination than is the case for Bonaventure (whose lesser role for sensory mediation in understanding is not necessarily truer to Augustine: the strange thing may be that Bonaventure exhibits both a reduction of a strong sense of participation and an ontologistic drift, encouraged by a voluntarist bias).

These conclusions suggest that, not only was de Lubac right to read Aquinas in terms of 'gift without contrast'

8. Schmutz, "La Doctrine mediévale."

(since this is the heart of the older *influentia* model), but also that this perspective was more specifically Thomistic than he realized.

In addition, it can be argued that other elements of a 'radicalization' of the *Surnaturel* thesis have Thomistic as well as patristic roots.

First of all, the spiritual dimension. As I mentioned earlier, in the *Summa Contra Gentiles* Aquinas presents the natural desire for the supernatural in the context of the general drive of all creatures towards the maximum possible unity with God that is consonant with their ontological status.[9] There must be a natural desire of spiritual creatures for beatitude, because intellectual creatures desire to return spiritually. Hence it would seem that, for Aquinas, there is no spiritual existence without grace (despite *Humani Generis*); this is confirmed by his statements that natural justice requires grace and that an intellectual creature without grace would be less than other creatures — because, one can infer, it would be radically disordered, wholly inappropriate, entirely inconvenient.

Secondly, there is the cosmic dimension. Aquinas discusses the particular mode of providence that God applies to the governance of spiritual creatures.[10] Here he appeals to the principle that everything must be ordered to an end, and says clearly that intellectual existence is the end of all non-intellectual created existence. The implication seems to be that, while God is the ultimate transcendent end, this end needs a 'representative' (like a political envoy) within

9. SCG III. 25. And see Chapter 2, note 10, above.
10. SCG III. 111-12.

the finite sphere. The ultimate Creator/created hierarchy can only be known about and mediated within the Creation if there is an analogical reflection of this hierarchy within the created order. As I indicated earlier, for Aquinas, not only is there an ontological difference between Being and beings at the top of the hierarchy, this difference is also somewhat reflected within ontic differences, forming indeed the principles of immanent hierarchic ordering. This is why the *influentia* model applies not just to divine causality, but also to finite causality which takes place through an emanative communication of forms.

Hence Aquinas argues that intellect properly governs the whole cosmos and that material things are there for the instrumental use of the intellect: they are the instruments of its art, such as when, to give his example, a man deploys an axe to give to some lumber the form of a bench that he has intellectually conceived. Spirits, though, are in turn ordered to the divine end. This then means that, whereas natural things are governed by immanent spirit, the latter as self-governing is *also* directly governed by something trans-cosmic and supernatural.

It follows that, for Aquinas as well as for de Lubac, spirit as such is in one sense "not merely natural." And it is for this reason that Aquinas indicates that the providential mode of dealing with spiritual creatures ultimately includes grace, since such creatures attain the "ultimate end" of knowing and loving God.[11]

Intellectual being reaches its proper divine end, uniquely "through its own operation" of intellect and will,

11. SCG. III [1]; 112. [3]. See also ST I. Q. 8, a3 resp.; Q. 65, a2.

and yet this needs the supplement of grace. How can this be so?

Well, the aforementioned passage in Aquinas shows that in part there is an analogical appeal to art: because the divine art creates spirits, God can 'instrumentalize', treat as his raw material, even mind. Therefore, grace, one might say, is 'the art of spirit-governing'. Just as human beings fulfill, for example, the proper potential of wood by making a table and yet wood would never 'tableize' by itself, but needs to be 'given' the form of table, so we are elevated (with the angels) by a divine art that does not abolish but fulfills our nature, though in a contingent, unexpected way.

The fact that Aquinas, while subordinating the intellectual/material distinction to the Creator/created divide, nonetheless sees the former as analogical to the latter, shows that he does not (anymore than Pico) really envisage the possibility of a cosmos not containing intellect. Cosmos requires the government of spirit; spirit is destined to be engraced; therefore in one sense every creature is already for and by grace. After all, how *could charis* be a less original or plenitudinous gift than *esse*?

But there is also evidence that Aquinas does not see the paradoxical ontology of the supernatural as an abrupt break with his normal ontology. This suggests that the entire structure of finite *esse* is a preparation for grace.

There is a parallel here between Aquinas's ontology of the finite and his theology of spirit. Just as in the latter case what is most fundamental and inward is received from without, so also in the former the most interior and basic aspect of a thing — its actuality — is entirely bestowed on it and is distinct from its specific properties, which (if anything) are alone what is proper to it. Indeed Aquinas always continued to speak of *esse* in some sense as 'an accident' of finite humanity. These fundamental essence-revising accidents are surely not purely Aristotelian.[12]

Nor, entirely, is Aquinas's understanding of nature and capacity. When justifying the idea that we can have a fundamental end beyond ourselves, Aquinas appeals to several natural examples: in particular the way hot water naturally provides warmth even though it has borrowed this capacity (by infusion) from fire, or the way the moon 'of itself' casts on us the borrowed light of the sun. Or again the way the oceans are naturally tidal, and yet this movement that is so proper to them — so basic to their entire ecology, we might say — is *entirely* due to the alien influence of the moon.[13] Hence certain analogues to the ontological-ontic causal order *within* the ontic order — whereby the higher 'flows into' the lower, giving it something of what is proper to it (for *nothing* in salt water is tidal movement) — are also seen by Aquinas as analogues for grace. He appeals, when discussing grace, to a Proclean ontology in which things are 'properly' raised above themselves to a new potential, not to a purely Aristotelian ontology in which things are confined for self-realization to an original, given potential.

Olivier Boulnois rightly stresses (as I said earlier) that in the end it was the arrival of Aristotelianism that created a crisis for the theology of grace and gave rise to the notion of pure nature. But he also shows how the category of 'art' in Aristotle was seen by mediaeval theologians as offering an

12. *De Potentia Dei*, Q. 5, a4 ad 3.
13. SCG III. 147 [3] [6]; *In Rom.* chap. 11, lect. 3.

exception to the confined notion of a fixed proper destiny. Fully grown trees are natural, but so are tables. I have shown above how appeal to this analogy is latent in Aquinas. But Aquinas appeals far more specifically to this analogy when explaining why it is appropriate that humanity's final end should not be within the reach of his given capacities.

Here he says that this lack is analogous to the human lack of natural armor and weapons.[14] Therefore Aquinas, like Pico later, evokes the Proteus theme in connection with grace. Lack of armor and weapons is more than compensated for by the human hand which has the capacity to produce (diverse and endlessly improving) weapons and armor, beyond any animal provision. Likewise, though we are not by nature turned to our last end, we have been given the gift of freedom which more than compensates for this lack, since it allows us to reach this end of our own volition (at one level). Since God alone governs our freedom and really turns our freedom towards him, freedom itself is here seen by Aquinas as the natural desire for the supernatural and even as obedience to grace. The gift of supernatural destiny *is* freedom, and it is the gift of our power to shape ourselves with true artistry. But in the same passage, Aquinas puts this supernatural *poesis* in the context of supernatural community: what we do through the influence of a friend we still do properly for ourselves (see the opening quotation in the Introduction, above). In this way, the vertical supplementarity of grace is, one could say, always mediated by the horizontal supplementarity of culture. Spirit is the paradoxical supplying of a poetic 'neces-

14. ST I-II. Q. 5, a5 ad I.

sary extra' because it is the recipient of the divine 'necessary extra'. Spirit supplements the cosmos with art since it is itself the divine artistic supplement.

For Aquinas, the cosmos where the waves are drawn by the moon is more a part of the creation — an infinite artifact — than it is part of nature, a given capacity. But divine creation includes the making of a work of art even out of artists. Such is the ultimate logic of the supernatural.

✛ 9 ✛

The Limit and the Renown
of Henri de Lubac

The drastic implications of Henri de Lubac's thought have only gradually come to light. Despite the indirectness and fragmentary character of his work, despite even his failure 'to do theology' or 'to do philosophy', his influence has now outlasted that of many once famous names. Arguably he is, along with Sergei Bulgakov, one of the two truly great theologians of the twentieth century.

Yet the *lacunae* in his work were partly shaped by his battles with authority. Is there not some contradiction here between his and von Balthasar's formal capitulation to papal authority on the one hand, and their ecclesiology on the other, which stressed the primacy of the sacramental influence of the bishops as eucharistic mediators? What of de Lubac's acknowledgment that papal power in the Middle Ages was falsely and permanently directed into an overly judicial and non-spiritual direction? And is there not some link to be made here with a failure to tackle the question of *patriarchy* and the rule of a male hierarchy? This question is not raised extrinsically, out of mere obeisance to fashion.

For latterly, both thinkers were wont to link the questions of the laity and of the Church with the question of the 'feminine'. Both of them adopted dualist models of the Church, distinguishing between a lay, receptive, mystical, cultural 'Marian' aspect and a more legal, regulative, intellectual, abstract 'Petrine' aspect.[1] But does not this duality ruin the inner structure of de Lubac's fundamental thought regarding the supernatural? If "the eternal feminine" is close to the natural desire for the supernatural, then it should be something paradoxically passive-active, and radically passive only in the sense that the most active human action is passive in relation to God. The Petrine function should also be, *as such,* Marian, in that, at the heart of its shaping activity it has also to do with a receptive giving birth again to Christ in the Eucharist, from whence (according to de Lubac) flows the body of the Church. If there is, indeed, a sheerly 'seminal' aspect, then this has more to do with non-human word and sacrament 'flowing into' the Church and informing all levels of its hierarchy, which are in various degrees and at various times, passive-active. A distinct 'passive' dimension to the Church sounds all too like a kind of collective 'supernatural existential' awaiting the extrinsic impact of male seminal authority. There is a failure here to think of all the

---

1. Henri de Lubac, *Paradoxes et Mystères de L'Eglise* (Paris: Aubier-Montaigne, 1967); *The Eternal Feminine,* trans. René Hague (London: Collins, 1971). See p. 95 for the comparison of Teilhard with Bulgakov. Hans Urs von Balthasar, *The Theology of Henri de Lubac* (San Francisco: Ignatius, 1991), pp. 105-21; *The Office of Peter and the Structure of the Church* [*Der antirömische Affekt*], trans. André Emery (San Francisco: Ignatius, 1986). See also Sergei Bulgakov, *Sophia: The Wisdom of God* (London: Lindisfarne, 1993), *passim.*

Church, in her bridal essence, as actively as well as passively Sophianic, as able potentially to meet the Bridegroom with an equal deified response since the Church, as the heavenly divine temple (Jerusalem who always abides with God above), is, one might venture to say, collectively, primordially and eschatologically enhypostasized by the Holy Spirit. Thus, according to the Apocalypse, the eternal Church is itself able to say to us "Come," to call us to deification, because its voice (and therefore its collective mind or personhood) is the voice of the Holy Spirit who also says to us "Come" (Apoc. 22:17). (This coincidence shows, incidentally, how we can say, with John of the Cross, Bérulle, and von Balthasar, that the Creation truly 'gives' glory back to God, as if adding something to him, without transgressing, like von Balthasar, the Creator/created divide.)

The prospectively equal mystical marriage of the Church with Christ reflects, then, the Spirit's eternal equality with the Son. Where the arrival of the Son and of *ecclesia* is seen more within this Russian perspective as the double descent of *Sophia,* there is no need to contrast a Christic-Petrine-Male active authority with a Marian-Female-Lay responsive one. (This double descent involves a descent of the *Logos* along with "the eternal humanity" — since the enhypostasized assumption of Christ's human nature by the eternal Logos must be an eternal fact which 'precedes' its origin in time — and the *Pneuma* along with the heavenly Jerusalem which is also an eternal fact for similar reasons.) If, on the Sophianic model, there still falls to the laity more the spiritual and 'natural' aspect and to the clergy the Christological and 'supernatural' one, this is no mere straightforward hierarchy, for the more the natural is 'raised' the more (as we have seen for de Lubac himself) it is actively re-invoked in its inherent natural character (the more we rise above the city, the more we return to govern it; the more we outgrow our ancestors, the more we renew their mythical intimations). The elevated laity should therefore not become quasi-clerical, but exercise their own governing roles in the Church while remaining in their diverse lay character, grounded in material, economic, political, military, and artistic operations.

If, for de Lubac, the supernatural is ultimately the 'eternal feminine' and the aporetic heart of Creation itself is 'not God/created God,' then it should follow that that which is Marian is not simply receptive, but 'actively receptive', just as the Mary of traditional Annunciation pictures who receives the angel is also the Mary who actively interprets the Scriptures which she peruses. Moreover, this aporetic heart is itself the showing forth outside of God of the heart of God himself as the interplay of donative difference. This interplay, this essence, is also the active/passive (infinitely dynamic yet infinitely replete) *Sophia* which names the Christian Godhead (in its unified essence) as 'goddess'.

De Lubac belonged to a particular generation and within that generation he was incomparable. Yet this generation scarcely prepared him to deal with all the many problematic dimensions of patriarchal authority that I have indicated above. Nevertheless, the radicalism of his own account of the supernatural suggests that it must be faced more critically than he ever imagined.

This issue aside, it is fair to say that contemporary Catholic theology, if it is to avoid both a liberalism and a conservatism that are predicated on the idea of an autonomous pure nature, needs to recover the authentic and more radical account of the natural desire for the supernatural as offered by de Lubac, both early and late in his career. This account is articulated in terms of spirit always orientated to grace, gift without contrast, the cosmos as lured by grace through humanity, unilateral exchange, and the link of grace with art. The vision is Catholic because it is Christological: totally specific only insofar as it is focused on the restoration of humanity in the God-Man, which allows again the universal reality of deified humanity. Never specifically consented to by de Lubac, but always exerting its own original lure, was Origen's vision of *apocatastasis:* the universal Christological salvation of spirits and through this, the eternal re-establishment of all things. *C'est du réel précis.*

INDEX

Academy of Gemistus Plethon, 50

Aesthetic compromise, 84-87. *See also* Thomistic criticisms of de Lubac's supernatural thesis

Aesthetics: the aesthetic compromise, 84-87; de Lubac's account of, 72-73; and grace/art analogy, 53-54, 88, 100, 108; and Thomistic criticisms of de Lubac's supernatural thesis, 79-87; von Balthasar on the transition from aesthetics to dramatics, 69-73; von Balthasar's division between fundamental and dogmatic theological, 73-74

Alexander of Hales, 97

Allegory and scriptural exegesis, 57-58

American life, de Lubac on, 22-23n.6

Analogia entis, 31, 73

Analogy: *analogia entis,* 31, 73; of grace and art, 53-54, 88, 100, 108; semantic concept of, 30-32, 31n.14; von Balthasar's restoration of de Lubac's concept of, 31

Aporia: and de Lubac's dualist model of the Church, 107; paradox of philosophy and theology, 5, 11-12; von Balthasar summary of de Lubac's, 11, 11n.14

Arendt, Hannah, 21

Aristotelianism, Aquinas and, 18-20, 23, 24, 29-30, 101-2

Augustine, St.: and de Lubac as Augustinian/Thomist, 89-90; and grace/deification, 16; and

Index

the *imago Dei*, 37; and the interior spark, 49; Jansenist/ Scotistic readings of, 33-34, 37; *natura pura* and Aquinas, 89, 94-95, 97
Augustinisme et Théologie Moderne (de Lubac), 8, 33-34, 48
Averroism, 59

Baius, 33-34
Barth, Karl, 31, 65-67, 74-76
Bérulle, Pierre, 14, 37-38, 38n.4; on Creation, 106; and heliocentrism, 23, 54; man in metaphysics of, 52, 53, 54-55; and *Pic de la Mirandole*, 38n.4, 43; von Balthasar on, 69
Blondel, Maurice, vi, 4, 64
Bonaventure, St., 70, 74, 89, 96-97
Bonhoeffer, Dietrich, 65
Bonino, Serge-Thomas, 80-81
Bouillard, Henry, 2, 24
Boulnois, Olivier, 101-2
Bresson, Robert, vii, 53
Bruaire, Claude, 43, 44-45, 47, 96
Buddhism, 6, 57
Bulgakov, Sergei, 14, 77-78, 104

Cajetan: and Aquinas on grace and the supernatural, 16-17, 28, 29-30, 35; and "potential for obedience," 64; and pure nature, 34
Calvin, John, 57
Catholicisme (de Lubac), 2
Causality. See *Influentia* model

Les chemins de Dieu (de Lubac), 44
Chenu, M.-D., 2
Church and "the eternal feminine," 105-7
Church authority, 6, 59-61, 105-7
Civitas Dei (Augustine), 59
Congar, Yves, 2
Convenientia, 84, 86
Corpus Mysticism (de Lubac), 6
Cosmic orientation to the supernatural, 53, 88, 108
Creation: Bérulle on, 106; and de Lubac's supernatural thesis, 39-40, 46-47, 52-53; gift of deification and, 39-40, 46-47; and *influentia* model of divine causality, 89-98, 99; ontological space for, 77; von Balthasar on, 77, 106

Daniélou, Jean, 2, 16
De Ente et Uno (Pico), 51
Deification: and de Lubac's supernatural thesis, 15-18, 23, 34, 39-40, 46-47; and gift of Creation, 39-40, 46-47; and grace in the West, 34; Greek/Latin patristic notions of, 16, 23; and *influentia* model, 91-92; late medieval/early scholastic break in grace and, 16-18
Deleuze, Gilles, 95
De Lubac, Henri, battles with ecclesiastical conservatism, 1-2, 6-7, 104-5; and effect of *Humani Generis*, 7-9; influence

Index

Index